Integrated Drawing Techniques

Integrated Drawing Techniques

Designing Interiors with Hand Sketching, SketchUp, and Photoshop®

Robert Philip Gordon

Columbia College Chicago
Chicago, Illinois

FAIRCHILD BOOKS
AN IMPRINT OF BLOOMSBURY PUBLISHING INC

B L O O M S B U R Y
NEW YORK • LONDON • OXFORD • NEW DELHI • SYDNEY

Fairchild Books
An imprint of Bloomsbury Publishing Inc

1385 Broadway	50 Bedford Square
New York	London
NY 10018	WC1B 3DP
USA	UK

www.bloomsbury.com

**FAIRCHILD BOOKS, BLOOMSBURY and the Diana logo are trademarks of
Bloomsbury Publishing Plc**

First published 2016

Library of Congress Cataloging-in-Publication Data
Gordon, Robert Philip.
Integrated drawing techniques : designing interiors with hand sketching, sketchup,
and photoshop / Robert Philip Gordon.
pages cm
ISBN 978-1-62892-335-3 (paperback)
1. Architectural drawing—Technique. 2. Architectural drawing—Data processing.
3. Interior architecture—Design. 4. Interior decoration—Design. I. Title.
NA2708.G66 2016
720.28'4—dc23
2015019184

ISBN: PB: 978-1-6289-2335-3
ePDF: 978-1-6289-2336-0

Typeset by Lachina
Printed and bound in China

CONTENTS

EXTENDED CONTENTS

When the designer designs, a lot has to happen, including identifying problems, clarifying functions, and shaping them into space plans. Design moves from the conceptual to the development phase. And now, more than ever before, design demands multiple graphic skills, including both freehand and digital imaging, as well as an ability to collaborate with other professionals using these tools.

In recent years, new techniques in digital rendering have increased the simplicity, speed, and affordability of many three-dimensional (3D) modeling and rendering programs, such as SketchUp and Photoshop. I believe that it is best to learn these skills on a project-based method, acquiring the techniques while designing a project. This book employs freehand drawing for the design concept. That means instead of learning freehand drawing, digital imaging, space planning, and conceptual design, as distinct from each other, we should use them simultaneously as integrated parts of the whole design process. This book provides a survey of the different techniques required for integrated drawing and design.

We can use both freehand drawing *and* digital programs such as SketchUp and Photoshop to design, as long as we know what their unique qualities are and when and how to use them. This book teaches a program of integrating drawing and design, by hand and computer, *as part of the design process, on a project-by-project basis*. I believe that designers do their best work, developing design and communicating it to clients, when they

take advantage of *integrating* hand rendering and digital technology, at the same time as they are developing the design.

Some say you can't design well unless you sketch and render by hand, because that process connects directly to your brain and designing instinct. Others say you're not keeping current unless you do digital rendering. But why choose? You can use them all.

Integrated Drawing Techniques: Designing Interiors with Hand Sketching, SketchUp, and Photoshop will show how all three of these techniques can be integrated and will give step-by-step exercise samples. This book presupposes some basic knowledge of freehand drawing and perspective construction, but it serves as a review of these techniques. It also compares these hand-drawn images to the new computer images demonstrated in the book. Additionally, it shows how freehand sketching, SketchUp modeling, and Photoshop rendering can be integrated for more effective presentations, as well as being used as a tool in the design of residential spaces.

Book Structure: How to Use This Book

In Part I, the book approaches design by first teaching or reviewing basic freehand drawing skills, first in black, white, and gray, and then in color. Examples of how freehand drawing is used in residential design are also shown.

Part II introduces digital techniques that can be used in conjunction with freehand drawing. Examples are shown of how digital techniques, such as SketchUp and Photoshop, can be integrated with freehand drawing for developing simple residential designs.

In Part III, residential design is developed using both freehand and digital tools for design and presentation. We examine single-family housing, townhouses, apartments, and mixed-use buildings. All aspects of residential space planning and furnishing are explored in detail.

Part IV explores the relationship among residential design, the landscape, and the surrounding neighborhood context, including commercial and transportation requirements. Freehand drawing, SketchUp, and Photoshop are combined with site photography and Google Earth to illustrate neighborhood plans.

There is also a gallery of residential and mixed-use design projects by prominent international artists, demonstrating the drawing techniques that were used to present them. These drawings are presented at the ends of corresponding chapters in the text, so that students can see how these techniques are used in professional practice.

ACKNOWLEDGMENTS

This book would not be possible without the influence and experience I have gained from my many colleagues in the professional and academic world, and from my students, who always ask the tough questions. Particular thanks goes to my colleagues who have contributed their work to this book in the Art Gallery sections:

- George Pappageorge
- Jean-Paul Viguier
- Ken Schroeder
- Patrick Rosen (who also contributed advice on site modeling)
- Daniel Heckman (my former graduate student)

These colleagues have all achieved the highest level of professional skill in their work, and it is an honor that they agreed to be part of this book.

I would also like to thank John Norquist, President of the Congress for the New Urbanism, for reading the chapters related to urbanism and offering his very keen advice. A special thanks to Joclyn Oats, Professor in the Art and Design Department of Columbia College Chicago, for her support and encouragement throughout all of my books. Also thanks to David Jameson, owner of the Architech Gallery in Chicago and the author of a scholarly book on Ianelli, who has exhibited my work in his gallery. And much appreciation to my colleagues who reviewed this book before publication: Your comments have definitely improved the book.

I want to also express my gratitude to my wife, Nancy Turpin, who read all the drafts of this book and looked at all of the images, offering encouragement and inspiration along the way. Joe Miranda and Edie Weinberg of Bloomsbury Publishing were also great collaborators in the development of this book.

DEDICATION

This book is dedicated to my son, Alex Gordon,
who loved drawing and making things.

Freehand Drawing and Rendering: Tools, Materials, and Techniques

Part I covers the use of hand-drawing techniques, including pencils and black ink pens in **Chapter 1**. It also includes an overview of colored pencils, markers, and watercolors in **Chapter 2**. **Chapter 3** reviews simple methods of perspective construction. These images serve as a comparison to the computer images that are used in subsequent chapters, and they are also useful images to import in the digital formats.

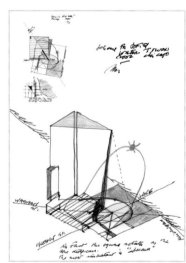
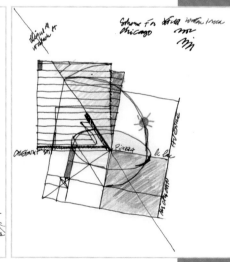

CHAPTER 1

Freehand Drawing: Pencil and Pen

Objectives

- Become familiar with the use of pencils, ink, and markers to make quick, accurate, and expressive lines
- Get the mind, body, and hand to relax and draw
- Develop the ability to use pencils, ink, and markers to make quick, accurate, and expressive line drawings
- Learn to use drawings and sketches to communicate with clients

Overview

This chapter shows the different types of pencils, pens, and markers available. We explore techniques of rendering shadows on line drawings and demonstrate how the techniques can be used individually or in combination for developing a drawing and designs. It is intended as a review of hand-drawn images for comparison to the computer-generated images, not as a method for teaching drawing.

Drawing Simple Lines

It all starts with a simple black line, drawn in pencil or ink. Most designers and architects start their conceptual design with this simple tool.

Depending on the designer's personality and ability, he or she will start to develop an individual style, for which his or her work will be known. Scribbling, note taking, and sketching on napkins or rolls of yellow sketch paper, using old wooden pencils sharpened into stumps, fountain pens, and Rapidograph pens are all part of the designer's toolkit.

Clients appreciate the freehand method of sketching because it shows an unfinished design that the client can help shape. This personal touch often helps establish a good rapport between designer and client, which can be maintained throughout the difficult days of budgeting, working drawings, and construction. The client will always remember the person who held the pen at the beginning of the concept and sketched the first few uncertain lines. Learning the techniques in this book is directed toward that end. The sketches aren't works of art in themselves, but they are an overall communication strategy.

Practice drawing every day. Completing a drawing per day will dramatically improve the skills of even a beginning sketcher. Choose a pencil or pen and a comfortably sized tablet, like the 6-by-9-inch Strathmore drawing pad, and carry it with you everywhere. Cafés are great places at which to draw. (You will see examples in Figures 1.16–1.20.)

Figure 1.1 Pencils. These pencils are commonly used and easily found: mechanical lead holder, Koh-i-noor Rapidomatic for 0.5 mm lead, 2H or H; office pencil, Waterman; No. 2 wood pencil; Prismacolor Black No. 935.

Figure 1.2a Pencil Line Weights: 2H, 0.5 mm; H, 0.5 mm; HB, 0.5 mm; No. 2 wood pencil; black Prismacolor.

Figure 1.2b Soft Pencil. Use for gradual shading.

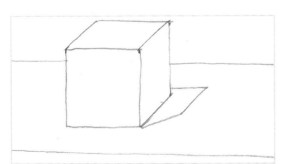

Figure 1.3 Cube outline in wood pencil.

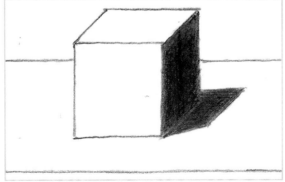

Figure 1.4 Cube black and white in Prismacolor.

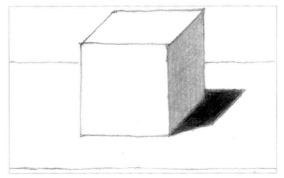

Figure 1.5 Cube black, white, and gray. No. 2 wood pencil with Prismacolor for cast shadow.

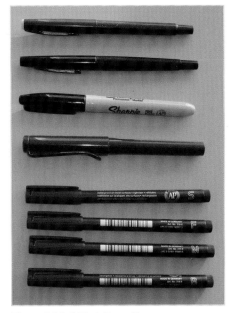

Figure 1.6 Felt Tech Pens. These pens are commonly used and easily found: Pilot Razor fine; Paper Mate Flair medium; Sharpie permanent marker; Lamy fountain pen; Staedtler permanent, superfine, fine, medium, bold.

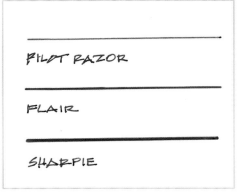

Figure 1.7 Felt pen lines.

Figure 1.8 Staedtler Felt Pen Lines: superfine, fine, medium, bold.

Figure 1.9 Micron Felt Pen Lines: micron 01 to 08.

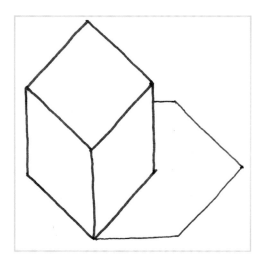

Figure 1.10 Cube outline in flair pen medium.

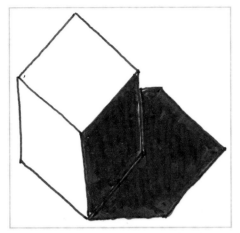

Figure 1.11 Cube black and white rendered in flair pen.

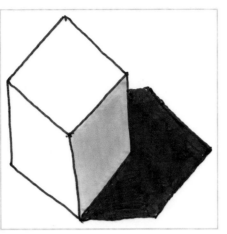

Figure 1.12 Cube in Black, White, Gray. Flair pen for outline and cast shadow, warm gray; medium (No. 5) Prismacolor marker for shaded face.

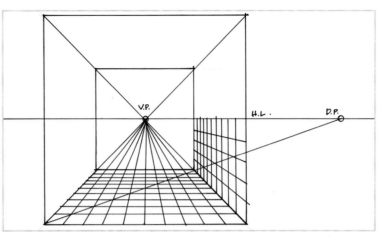

Figure 1.13 Interior of Cube With Grid in Flair Pen. This diagram also begins to show how to construct a simple interior perspective.

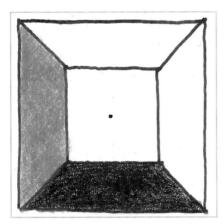

Figure 1.14 Interior of Cube Shaded Black, White, Gray. Outline in flair pen. Shading in Prismacolor pencils: shaded face French gray 50 percent, cast shadow black.

Figure 1.15 Rapidograph pen, 2.5, India ink with Strathmore plate paper and carrying cases. India ink is a very dark, permanent black that contrasts well, especially on smooth plate paper. However, these pens tend to clog and must be cleaned frequently.

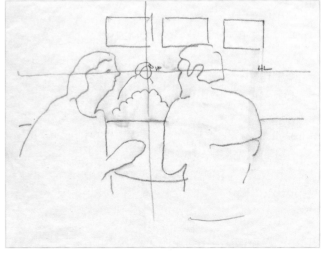

Figure 1.16a Couple in café, Mouffetard, Paris. Pencil sketch. Rough outline in pencil, noting horizon line at eye level.

Figure 1.16b Create an ink version of this drawing.

Figure 1.16c Create a *rendered* version of this drawing.

Figure 1.17 Crowded café, Paris, pen sketch.

Figure 1.18 Café Rostand, Paris, pen sketch.

Figure 1.19 "Looking for a Job" pen sketch. Reading *Le Figaro* want ads in café.

Always give your drawings a title and date and sign them. They will become a personal diary. Make notes of what people around you are saying. This will help you learn how to annotate your design sketches. Include notes and thoughts you may have on projects you are currently working on. You will be able to use them in the studio.

Figure 1.20 Girls writing and dreaming, pen sketch, Paris.

KEY TERMS

Wood pencils: Old-fashioned No. 2 wood pencils used for rough hand sketching

Mechanical pencils: Technical pens, Pentel, or Rapidograph for India ink used for hand sketching

Various line weights: A line is a mark made by a pencil, pen, marker, or other writing instrument. Variety of the thickness of lines creates interest in a drawing.

EXERCISES AND PRACTICE

1. Stretch and breathe deeply before you start to work. It will help relax your body and mind.
2. Scribble whenever and wherever you can. Make doodles. They don't have to have meaning.
3. Start a daily sketchbook. Make at least one sketch a day from your daily life.
4. Make notes of what you see and include them in the sketchbook.

ART GALLERY

A selection of line drawings by architects Jean-Paul Viguier Architecte of Paris and Ken Schroeder of SMNG in Chicago. These are drawings by professionals who are world leaders in design and technology, and yet who conceive their projects with simple, elegant hand sketches at the very outset. (See captions for greater detail.)

Jean-Paul Viguier Architecte, Paris

Jean-Paul Viguier's practice consists of many sophisticated technological buildings. He begins with elegant line sketches in his sketchbooks, sometimes enhanced with colored pencils.

Jean Paul Viguier, by Laurent Greilsamer, published by Editions Tallandier, 2013. A book of drawings that were used to produce the recent work by this noted French architect. This book illustrates the importance of freehand sketches in the development of highly sophisticated and technical buildings. M. Viguier explains his use of the sketches in the design process and the historical context of drawing in the age of computer rendering.

Following are sketches from his book:

Figure G1.2 C3D Head office.

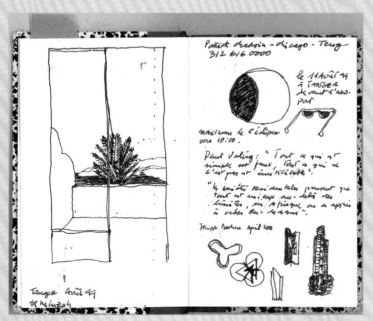

Figure G1.1 "Drawing Is the Architect's Handwriting." Sketchbook with sunglasses, landscape, objects.

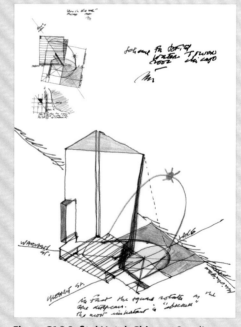

Figure G1.3 Sofitel Hotel, Chicago. Sun diagram.

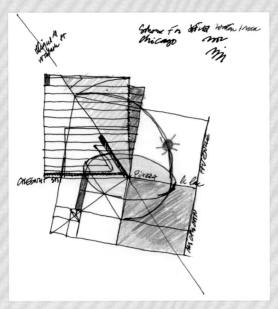

Figure G1.4 Sofitel Hotel, Chicago. Site diagram.

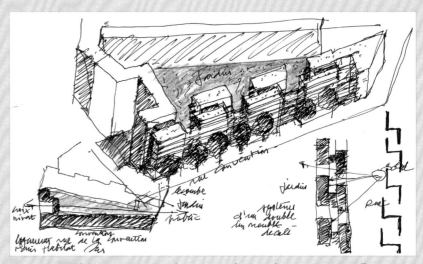

Figure G1.5 Mid-Rise Housing Development, 15th Arrondisement, Paris. Offset stepped to maximize views.

Figure G1.6 Metropole 19. Sketch of walkway between buildings from below.

Figure G1.7 Curving Pathway, Pont Du Gard Archaeology Museum. Connects museum and parking to ancient Roman aqueduct.

Figure G1.8 SFR, Gaz de France, Saint Denis. Street façade with terraces.

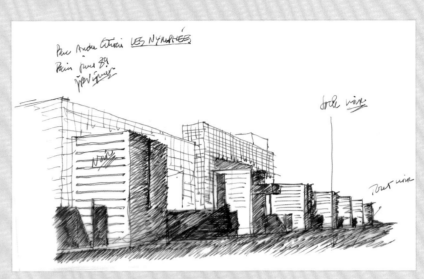

Figure G1.9 Parc Citroen, Paris. Row of seven fountains.

Figure G1.10 Hospital in Southwest France.

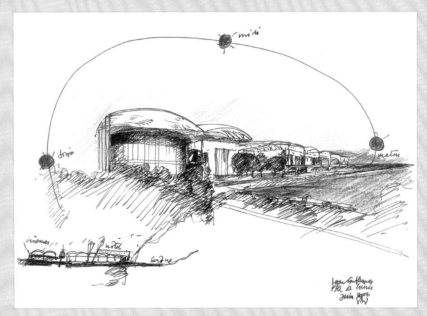

Figure G1.11 Sun diagram; commercial center, Lyon.

SMNG Architects

Ken Schroeder of SMNG architects designs schools and public buildings. His simple single-line drawings are the inspiration for the finished buildings, which are shown alongside of the sketches here and in **Chapter 2**.

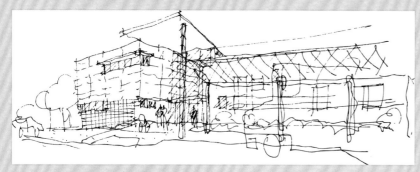

Figure G1.12 Langston Hughes Elementary School (Courtesy Ken Schroeder).

Figure G1.13 Langston Hughes Elementary School (Photo courtesy John Faier).

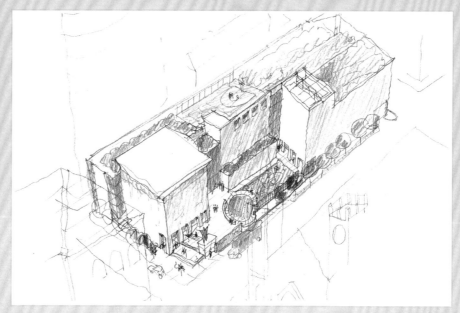

Figure G1.14 Ogden International School (Courtesy Ken Schroeder).

Color Drawing and Rendering: Working with Mixed Color Media

Objectives

- Explore the various media available, including markers, colored pencils, and watercolors.
- Show how these media can be integrated and used together.

Overview

This chapter explores the various color media that are readily available, such as colored pencils, markers, and watercolors. Practice using markers and colored pencils. See how they can be integrated and used together. Markers bring a certain smoothness and coverage, whereas colored pencils can show textures and blending of colors with markers, and can make some areas of the drawing more saturated.

Multiple Techniques for Drawing and Rendering in Color

As you become more skilled in line drawing, you will probably aspire to a greater level of rendering in color. You will want to add color to your drawings. Make your life and your drawings more colorful and lively. Color can be controversial, because there are no strict rules on what makes a pleasant color scheme. There are, of course, color theories, color wheels, color systems, and various theories of design. There is also a difference between color on paper and the color of light on a screen. Color theory is not within the scope of this book, but it will affect everything we do. Many books are available on this subject, and the serious student should read some of them. We will show what tools are available and how they can be applied to line drawings to create a full and rich color rendering.

Let's look in detail at the tools available to you and how you can use them. First, we will use colored pencils. They are a simple and inexpensive way to add color to your drawings. The Prismacolor brand is reliable, inexpensive, and readily available. Figure 2.1 shows a flat box of colored pencils arranged so that most are visible at a glance. Keep them organized so they will be easy to find when you are working. Keep cool colors like blues and blue-greens on one side, warm colors like reds and oranges on the other, and the neutrals like some greens, yellows, and grays in the middle. Figure 2.2 shows how these pencils look on a sheet of paper.

Figure 2.1 Colored Pencils. Box of assorted Prismacolor colored pencils. Flat box keeps them visible. Organize cool blues and grays on the left, medium greens and yellows in the center, and warm reds and browns to the right.

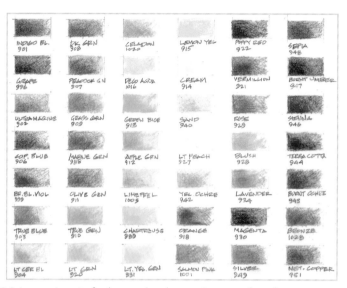

Figure 2.2 An assortment of colors rendered on tracing paper for reference.

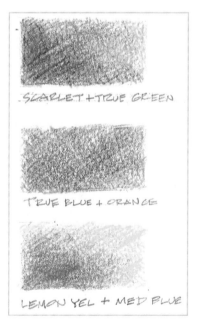

Figure 2.3 Blended colored pencils, mixing complementaries. Cross-hatch the dark color over the light, leaving white spaces for blending. This method gives a richer color scheme than using simply one color.

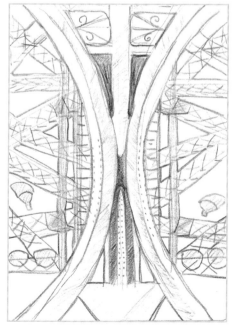

Figure 2.4 Eiffel Tower, Colored Pencil Sketch. A quick color study. Although it is not exactly accurate, it's useful for defining cool and warm areas for later rendering.

Use paper that is especially suited for colored pencil drawing, like the Strathmore 400 series or some plain bonds with slight textures.

The next tool to explore is markers. Again, Prismacolor makes a sound, reliable product, but some others are on the market as well. Try them and see which ones you like best. As with colored pencils, keep your markers organized. It is recommended to use plastic bags for the different color groups, as shown in Figures 2.5 to 2.11. The plastic bags keep the markers fresh as well as organized.

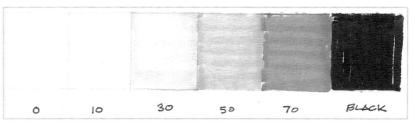

Figure 2.6 Gray Scale, 10, 30, 50, 70, Black. Range of shades useful for contrast drawings.

Figure 2.5 Gray Markers. Warm gray Prismacolor markers: 10 percent to 90 percent and black. Grays are good for blocking out contrast in a drawing and can be overdrawn with colored pencils to blend different colors and values. You don't need them all.

Figure 2.7 Brown and Tan Prismacolor Markers: terra cotta, bronze, clay, sand, sienna, sepia, light umber, dark umber, flagstone green, flagstone blue, flagstone red, brick white. These earth colors provide a basis for many building materials: brick, wood, stone, tile. They can be highlighted with colored pencils.

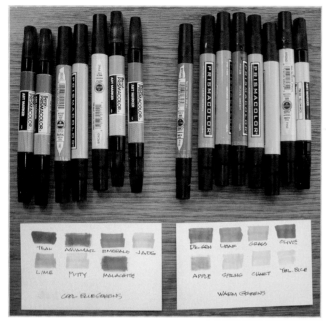

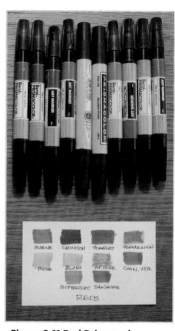

Figure 2.8 Green Prismacolor Markers. Cool: teal, aquamarine, emerald, jade, lime, putty, malachite. Warm: dark green, leaf, grass, olive, apple, spring, chartreuse, yellow bice. Greens are a source for landscape and nature colors. Many rooms are influenced by the reflections of trees through the windows and can in turn influence color schemes.

Figure 2.9 Yellow and Tan Prismacolor Markers: sand, cream, yellow ochre, yellow orange, canary yellow, deco orange, mustard yellow and light sand. Mustard colors are good for lightening a drawing and providing contrast to the darker colors. They tend to be in the neutral range of color.

Figure 2.10 Blue Prismacolor Markers: ultramarine, grape, imperial violet, light cerulean blue, cloud blue, blue slate. Light cerulean blue is a good basis for skies, but it must be used carefully, because it can be streaky and calls attention to itself. It's better to use watercolors, pastels, or colored pencils for skies. Detail to follow with examples.

Figure 2.11 Red Prismacolor Markers: rubine, crimson, scarlet, vermilion, pink rose, blush pink, apple blossom, Chinese vermilion, bittersweet, sanguine. These colors add warmth to rooms. Many designers prefer warm color schemes to engage the residents.

Figure 2.12 Watercolors. A selection of watercolor tubes. Choose the best quality, because they will last a long time. Just add water when they dry out.

Figure 2.13 A Watercolor Palette by Michael Wilcox. A useful way of organizing and mixing colors.

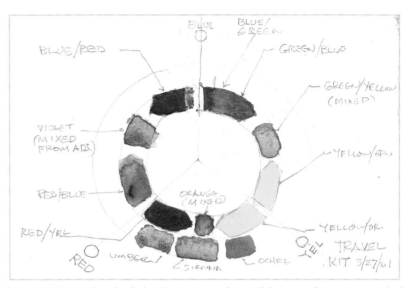

Figure 2.14 Watercolor wheel, showing primary colors and their complementaries applied to watercolor paper.

Figure 2.15 A Selection of Brushes. Broad flat brushes are useful for applying washes to large areas. Fine brushes are used for painting details. Set them on a practical bamboo brush carrier.

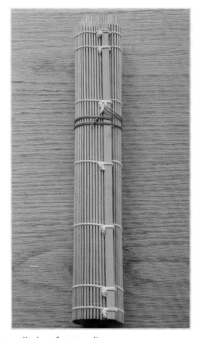

Figure 2.16 Brush carrier, rolled up for traveling.

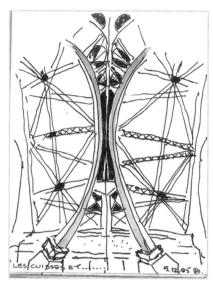

Figure 2.17 Couple in Mouffetard Café. Made from line drawing in previous chapter, **Figure 1.16a.** The drawing was photocopied onto acetate. The image was transferred onto watercolor paper with transfer paper. Watercolor was loosely applied. Then the acetate drawing was placed on top. This yields a rich mixture of strict line technique with looser watercolor.

Figure 2.18 Eiffel Tower "Cuisses" (thighs). Ink sketch with light watercolor wash.

Figure 2.19 Eiffel Tower. Site study of front façade. Ink sketch with watercolor wash. The ink sketch was made on site, and the watercolors were added later in the studio. The red depicts the warm, sunny areas, with the blue depicting shadows. This sketch was later used for a detailed watercolor and even a metal plate etching.

Figure 2.20 View Through Window, Paris. India ink on plate stock.

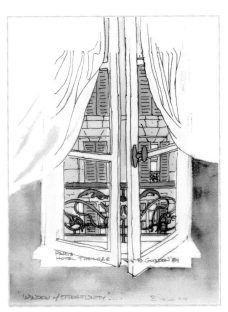

Figure 2.21 View Through Window, Paris. Acetate face, watercolor underlay. The warm color of the interior window frame and the flowing drapes help create a feeling of warmth in the room and distance from the building across the street. The watercolor paper is larger than the drawing, permitting an amplification of the image in context of the room.

Figure 2.22 View Through Window, Dijon. India ink on Strathmore paper, kid finish. The window shows the distance between the room and the outdoor image of the stone arch.

Figure 2.23 View Through Window, Dijon. India ink on Strathmore paper, kid finish, watercolor wash. The additional watercolor adds warmth to the room, as well as a separation from the outdoor image.

Watercolors can be used to effectively cover large areas of paper. They come in tubes and last a long time, so get a good-quality brand. Also, get a nice assortment of brushes, including very wide 1-inch to 1½-inch brushes for covering large areas. See an example of a painting of Mont St. Michel in Figures 2.26 and 2.27. After completing transferring a line drawing in pencil or pen to the watercolor paper, spread a thin, light layer of watercolor over the entire area of the paper. Use

pale lemon yellow to show the sunlight behind the clouds, if it will be a warm color scheme. This will provide a unifying tone for the entire drawing. Then apply intermediary layers, such as greens and blues in the case of Mont St. Michel. Begin to develop the darker areas, using Payne's Gray in the upper right to render the clouds. Finally, fill in the darker areas with more saturated colors, and you will complete a quickly rendered and colorful drawing.

Figure 2.24 Mont Saint Michel. A line drawing of the historic monument in Normandy, made on site. Pen was Rapidograph 2.5 drawn on Strathmore plate stock.

Figure 2.25 Grid overlay (1/2-inch square) over original ink drawing.

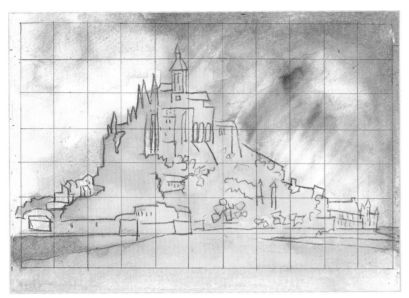

Figure 2.26 Draw a grid on watercolor paper using a pencil, increasing size to 1-inch square. This will result in a 9-by-12-inch drawing. Then start to sketch the image from Figure 2.26, coordinated with the original grid, and begin applying base layers in watercolors.

Figure 2.27 Final watercolor of Mont St. Michel.

Figure 2.28 The light blue background shows the light towers in a late afternoon scene.

Figure 2.29 The dark blue background shows evening lighting.

Figure 2.30 Laser light arch sculptures can be shown well on blue background paper, this one at dusk.

Material Swatches

Students are asked to copy material samples by hand, with markers and colored pencils. This helps them get a feel for the depth of the materials and aids them in final selection. When there is a delay in obtaining original samples for a concept presentation, students will feel confident in creating their own version by hand. Shown here are the following samples and the media used to produce them. (Prismacolor markers and colored pencils were used.)

Figure 2.31 Slate (courtesy of Sasha Montes)

- Light umber
- Green tea
- French gray 20%, 40%, and 10%
- Cool gray 20%
- Putty

Figure 2.32 Black marble (courtesy of Tomoe Yunoki)

- Black marker
- White colored pencil

Figure 2.33 White marble (courtesy of Dahlia Zarour)

- Gray, sand, cream, and white colored pencils

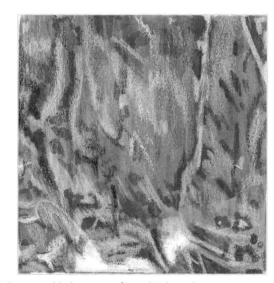

Figure 2.34 Green marble (courtesy of Nayeli Talavera)

Markers:
- Dark green
- Green 158
- Yellow green

Colored pencils:
- Black
- White
- Cool gray

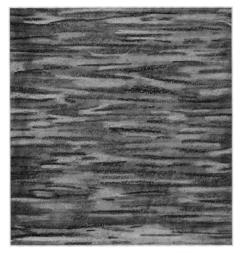

Figure 2.35 Walnut (courtesy of Nayeli Talavera)

Markers:
- Dark brown
- Cream

Colored pencils:
- Cream
- Sienna brown
- Ginger root
- Brun fonce
- Brun ombre clair

Figure 2.36 Dark oak (courtesy of Sasha Montes)

Markers:
- Light umber
- Sienna brown
- Light brown
- Goldenrod

Figure 2.37 Cherry wood (courtesy of Dahlia Zarour)

Markers:
- Cool gray 30%
- Sand
- Dark brown
- Sienna brown

Colored pencils:
- Burnt ochre
- Sienna brown
- Seashell pink
- Sepia
- Light umber
- Peach beige
- Dark brown

Figure 2.38 Maple (courtesy of Tomoe Yunoki)

Markers:
- Sand
- Cream
- Warm gray 20%

KEY TERMS

Prismacolor pencils: Recommended brand of colored pencils for colored sketches. They are wax based rather than graphite based and will not smear easily, so you can show the strokes.

Gray markers: Grays are good for blocking out contrast in a drawing and can be overdrawn with colored pencils to blend colors and values.

Gray scale: Range of shades are useful for contrast on drawings.

Watercolors: Come in tubes in a wide variety of colors and can be used effectively to cover large areas of paper.

Brushes: Broad flat brushes are used for applying washes to large areas and fine brushes for painting details.

ART GALLERY

Figure G2.1 Robert Gordon of RGArchitecture/Planning of Chicago designed this single-family residence in 1976, before the age of computer renderings. The renderings are entirely colored pencil sketches of the exteriors. South View. Preliminary Concept Sketch. Later, a larger porch was added across the entire façade. The house is oriented toward a large garden on the south.

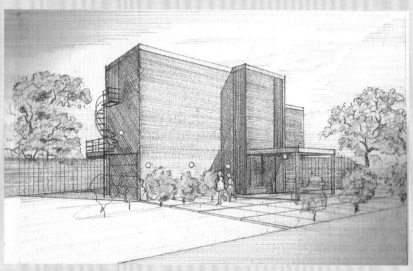

Figure G2.2 North View. The house turns its back on the driveway and is insulated from the cold north winds of Chicago.

Figure G2.3 Building entry (Courtesty Ken Schroeder).

Figure G2.4 Art Wall, courtesy of SMNG Architects.

Figure G2.5 Interior lobby.

Figure G2.6 Ogden International School (Courtesy David Parisi, dPict Visualization, Inc.).

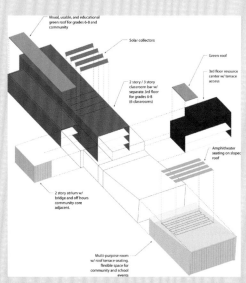

Figure G2.7 Exploded axonometric "Kit of Parts."

Figure G2.8 Linked annex (Courtesy David Parisi, dPict Visualization, Inc.).

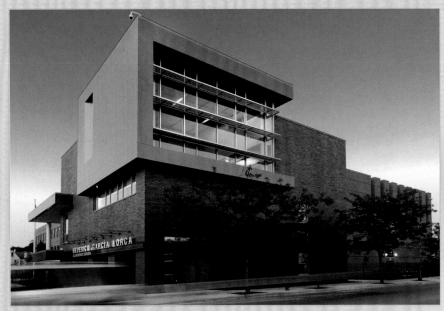

Figure G2.9 Lorca (Photo courtesy John Faier).

Figure G2.10 Skinner School (Photo courtesy John Faier).

Perspective

VANISHING POINT

> You thought it was just a pencil dot
> Art students made in the middle of the canvas…
> But here I am at the vanishing point, looking back at everything
>   as it zooms toward me…
> I am a catcher behind the home plate of the world…
> I watch the history of architecture narrow down
> To nothing…
> Every monument since Phidias converges on this speck…
> I have reached the heaven of geometry
> Where every line…aspires to go.

(Billy Collins, *The Apple That Astonished Paris,* The University of Arkansas Press, 2006, p. 3)

Objectives

- Review the basic techniques of one-point and two-point perspective.
- Quickly sketch ideas and visualize design concepts.

Overview

For a professional presentation, you must be very careful that all of the perspectives you use respect proper horizon lines, diagonal lines, and vanishing points. In perspective drawing, you must become very intimate with the vanishing point. Whether drawing freehand from life, constructing it with a triangle and T-square, or drawing it with a computer, you must employ a thorough knowledge of the rules of perspective for every rendering. It should become second nature, which is achieved through much practice and experience. Nothing makes your presentation more amateurish than incorrect use of horizon lines, diagonals, and vanishing points in your perspectives. In this chapter, we discuss a few of the basic rules that you can use for whatever media you choose. Trace and analyze photographs to determine horizon lines, diagonals, and vanishing points. This will help you develop the skills necessary for freehand and accurate perspective sketching. This chapter is intended as a review or a primer of hand-drawing techniques of perspective construction and the key terms. It can be used to compare hand-drawing perspective to the SketchUp method of modeling by computer, not as a stand-alone method for teaching hand-drawing perspective.

You should be aware that the full technique of hand-drawing perspective is considerably more complex than we are showing here. The technique is originally attributed to Brunelleschi, in 1413.[1]

We can't possibly go into that much detail in this chapter. This basic understanding will help you understand quickly any errors that may have been made with a perspective drawing. It will also serve as a guide to construct perspectives in SketchUp, because you will already have experience in setting up the point of view.

One-Point Perspective

One-point perspectives are the most useful for an interior designer and also the simplest to learn and use. You can elevate them from floor plans and set them up directly from elevations. Viewing a room interior straight on allows you to draw the elevation to scale and project space forward. Figures 3.1 to 3.9 show examples of setting up the one-point perspective, adding furniture, and then rendering it. A basic preliminary understanding of perspective would be useful for these exercises.

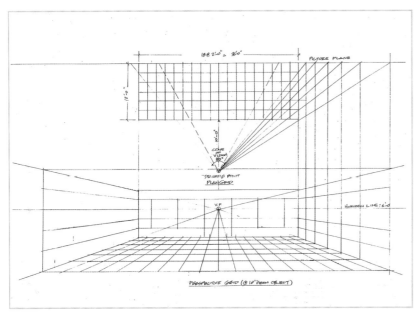

Figure 3.1 Set up a grid for constructing one-point perspectives.

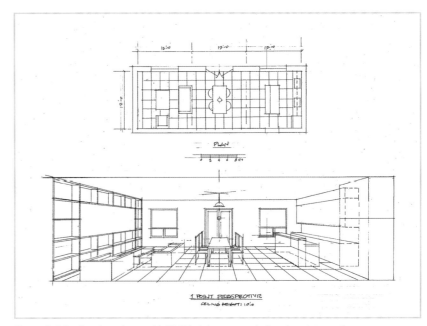

Figure 3.2 Set furniture into grid. Wall heights are scaled at the picture plane.

1. For a thorough history of perspective, read Martin Kemp, *The Science of Art* (New Haven, CT: Yale University Press, 1990), 9.

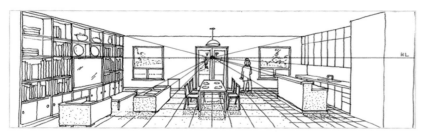

Figure 3.3 Render the furniture with lines. Use stippling, a dotted pattern, to indicate shadows.

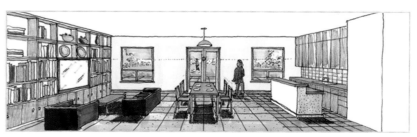

Figure 3.4 Render the furniture in color with markers and colored pencils.

Figure 3.5 Set up traditional living room furniture for a color rendering of a simple one-point perspective. Alternatively, modern furniture or other styles can be set up quickly using the same grid.

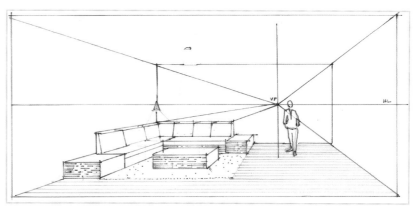

Figure 3.6 Seating Area. Using the previous method, construct a one-point perspective. Show only the important main features. First draw the horizon line, at 5 feet 0 inches high. Then draw a vertical line at the viewer's location. The intersection of these two lines will form a vanishing point. All diagonal lines emanate from this point and form the room. Remember, the back wall (the picture plane) is drawn at true scale, so you can measure the furniture from that back wall. Place a figure and some detail in this drawing to guide you. You can also show lighting where you want it. In this case, place a reading light in the corner where the seating comes together. Show a ceiling light above the coffee table.

Figure 3.7 Trace over the constructed perspective. You can use freehand or a straight edge, or a combination of the two. The pillows and the figure were drawn freehand. Add a pair of French doors and a picture over the seating area.

Figure 3.8 Value Drawing. Determine the light and dark areas determined by the interior lighting and slightly around the door. Render the values you want to establish in the color rendering.

Figure 3.9 Color Rendering of Seating. Render the image with markers and colored pencils. Be careful to leave areas around the lights uncolored. Use sand marker for the edges of the benches and sand for the flooring. A true green colored pencil is used for the fabric, complemented and cross-hatched with poppy red and copper. This yields a texture to the fabric. A pink rose marker is used as a base for the carpet. Blend a light shade of true green colored pencil to pick up the color of the fabric. Then cross-hatch with copper to tie in the warmth of the wood floor and benches.

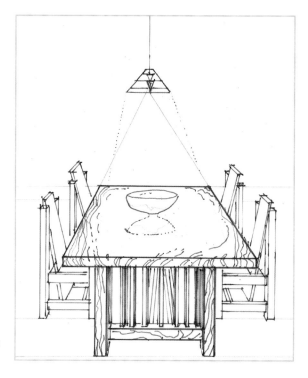

Figure 3.10 Prairie Style Table and Chairs. Waxed and polished wood. One-point perspective with hanging stained glass lamp. Indication of light area and reflection as basis for color rendering.

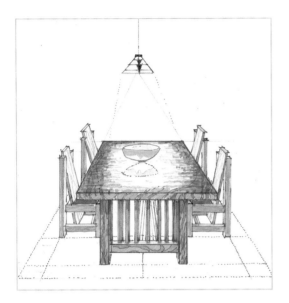

Figure 3.11 Color rendering of table and chairs, one-point perspective, showing light area and reflection of bowl. Notice that bowl reflection is lighter than the original. Markers: bronze, sand, and cream. Use cream colored pencil to tone and white colored pencil to lighten. True green for bowl, with Deco green colored pencil for reflection. Poppy red colored pencil for lamp highlights. Warm gray light, 20%, for carpet, with cream colored pencil to warm it up and show some reflected light. Metallic copper colored pencil for wood grain.

Two-Point Perspective

The two-point perspective is asymmetrical and more dynamic than the one-point perspective. It is also better for showing exteriors, because it shows the space around the building. All of the other rules of inserting furniture and determining heights apply, but there is only one true measuring line, where the plan intersects the picture plane.

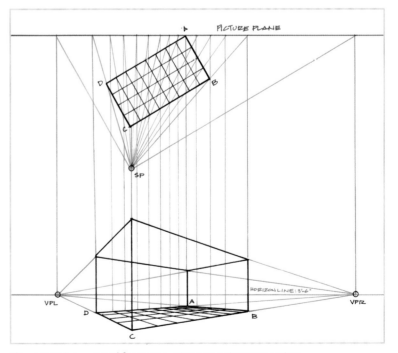

Figure 3.12 Set up a grid for constructing two-point perspectives.

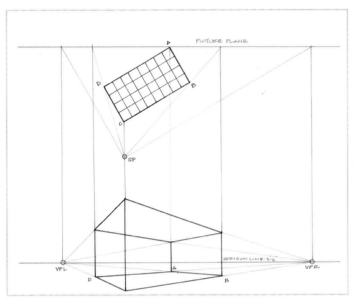

Figure 3.13 This grid places the viewer outside of the space and can be used for interiors and exteriors.

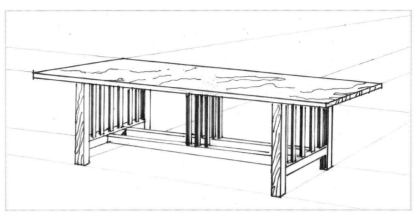

Figure 3.14 Prairie style table, two-point perspective.

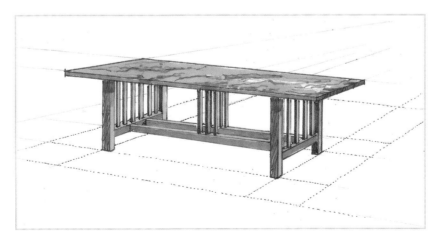

Figure 3.15 Color rendering of table, two-point perspective. Markers: bronze base with light umber shadows and sand for streaking. Metallic copper colored pencil for wood grain. The dotted lines show the potential for carpeting, although they are left uncolored for this rendering.

KEY TERMS

Vanishing point: The point or points on a drawing toward which all diagonal lines converge.

One-point perspective: A drawing with only one vanishing point.

Two-point perspective: A drawing with two vanishing points.

Horizon line: The horizontal line that represents the viewer's eye level.

Picture plane: The plane, generally at the back of a perspective, upon which all dimensions are measurable.

Measuring line: The vertical line on a two-point perspective that is measurable.

Point of view: The vantage point of the viewer, both in relation to the floor plan and to the vertical height.

EXERCISES AND PRACTICE

1. Make digital photographs and print them. Trace all of the diagonal lines to see where they intersect. That should show you the horizon line.

2. In your sketchbook, draw a series of sketches from life each day that show only the horizon line, vanishing points, and a vague outline of the room or building. Take two minutes for each of these sketches.

3. Render these sketches quickly with the techniques shown in **Chapters 1 and 2**. You should only be showing basic modeling and shading, not details. Take 2 to 5 minutes for this rendering.

4. Draw one sketch per day that is more finished, taking a maximum of 15 to 20 minutes each. Draw them in sketchbooks over a sustained period. Title them, sign them, and date them. Leave the horizon line and vanishing point(s) on the sketches for future reference. After three to six months, you will notice a dramatic increase in your skills, which will become second nature. You will have a diary that you can continue for the rest of your life. Believe it or not, it doesn't take long to make thousands of drawings. This work will help you set up models in your SketchUp renderings as well.

PART II

Digital Rendering

Chapter 4 introduces basic SketchUp techniques and tools for modeling. **Chapter 5** then introduces the basic tools and techniques for finishing and rendering in Photoshop. We show how SketchUp views can be saved as jpegs and converted to Adobe Photoshop, where they can be edited, enhanced, and merged with backgrounds and other images. Finally, **Chapter 6** shows ways to integrate freehand sketching into both of these digital programs through a series of simple projects. It also demonstrate how freehand drawing can be used to study the design by tracing SketchUp models.

CHAPTER 4

SketchUp Techniques

Objectives

- Become familiar with the basic menus and tools of the SketchUp program.
- Learn the most important tools for using SketchUp, by using each tool as part of the technique for developing a simple studio, and then turning the studio into a one-bedroom house.
- Quickly model 2D hand drawings into a 3D format for design development and further rendering.

Overview

In this chapter you will learn the basic techniques for modeling in SketchUp. You should be able to quickly construct models of specific sizes and then orbit around to different views. You can then save these views as jpegs and open them in Photoshop, which is discussed in the next chapter.

Starting to Use SketchUp

SketchUp is a program that is easy to start. It's very user-friendly and clear. It includes useful tutorials so that you can start using it almost immediately. However, even the free SketchUp download can be developed into very detailed and complicated scenarios that take time to learn. In this chapter, we introduce you to the basic tools while designing a simple studio. Then a bedroom/bathroom wing will be added to complete a simple house. In later chapters, more techniques and tools will be used for other models.

You will select a view to start with. Go to **Camera**>**Standard Views** and choose. It can be a plan or elevation. Scroll down and choose the **Perspective** or **Two-Point Perspective** model. (See Figure 4.2.) You will then be ready to start drawing. Choose the rectangle tool. Note the dimension window in the lower right corner where you insert specific dimensions. The default number is in inches, so you must note feet (say 12 feet). (See Figures 4.3 and 4.4.)

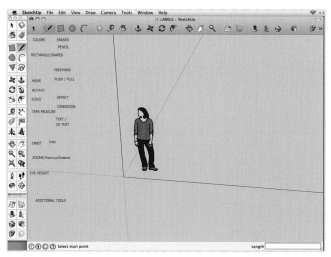

Figure 4.1 Startup Page. This is the first image on the screen when you open SketchUp. The most important tools for designers are labeled. The horizontal toolbar at top repeats the tools. At the very top is the Main Menu, showing Edit, View, Draw, Camera, and Window.

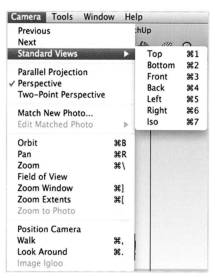

Figure 4.2 Camera Menu>Standard Views>Top (plan), Front (elevation), or other choices.

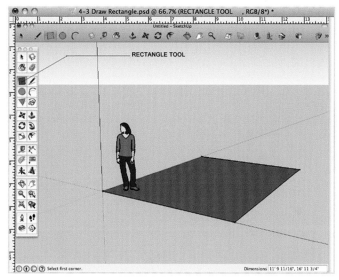

Figure 4.3 Draw a rectangle of indeterminate size, using the Rectangle tool. Notice the box in the lower right-hand corner. This will enable you to fix specific dimensions to the rectangle. Type in a dimension for the x-axis, then a comma, then the y-axis. We use the Rectangle tool instead of the Line tool because this establishes a 3D view.

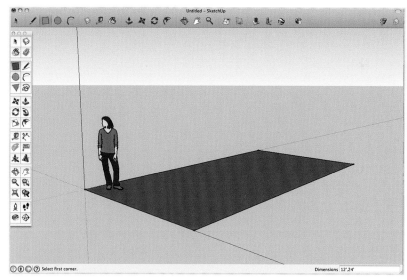

Figure 4.4 Draw a dimensioned rectangle of 12 feet wide by 24 feet deep. This footprint of 288 square feet will be used to develop a SketchUp plan for a studio with a living/dining/kitchen space. (A bedroom/bathroom suite will be developed in Part III, Residential Design with Integrated Media.) This plan demonstrates most of the basic tools for using SketchUp.

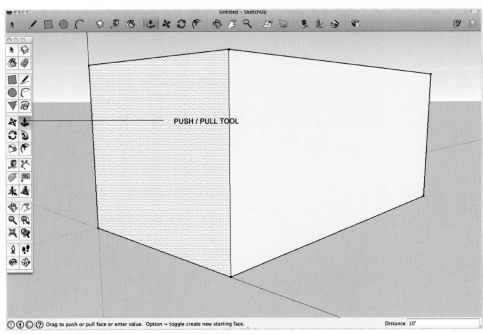

PUSH / PULL TOOL

Figure 4.5a Use the Push/Pull tool to extrude the rectangle to a height of 10 feet.

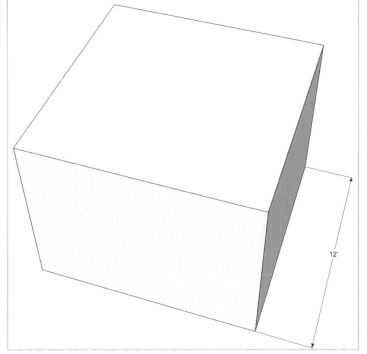

Figure 4.5b Remember the hand-drawn "cubes" (pencil and ink) from
Chapter 1? Here's how the same cube looks in SketchUp, drawn in perspective.

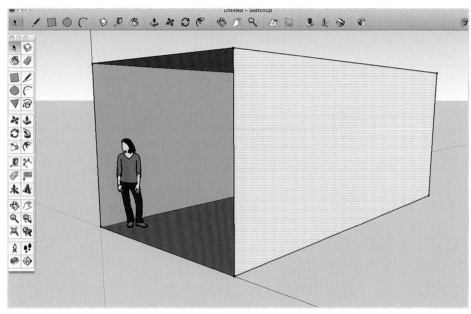

Figure 4.6 Select Front wall and press Delete.

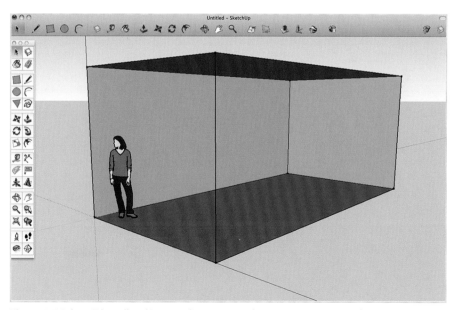

Figure 4.7 Select Side wall and press Delete. You now have an open 3D view of a room-sized space, showing the interior.

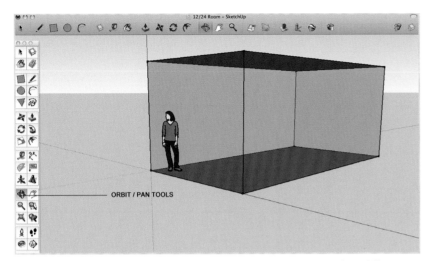

Figure 4.8a Use the Orbit tool and the Drag (Hand) tool to view images from different points.

Figure 4.8b Orbit to right. You will see the exterior wall on the right and a different view of the room.

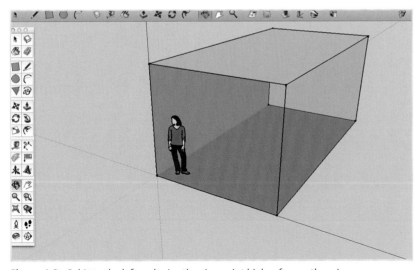

Figure 4.8c Orbit to the left and raise the viewpoint higher for another view.

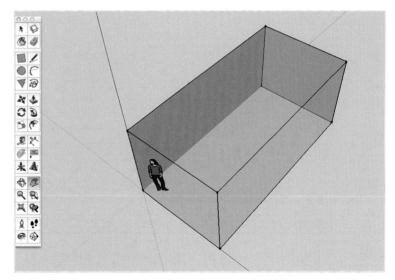

Figure 4.8d Raise the vantage point substantially higher for a bird's-eye view of the room. Use the Drag (Hand) tool to drag the image where you want it on the screen.

The **Tape Measure** tool is very useful for measuring distances in the drawing. It can also be used for creating guidelines. (See captions for details.)

The **Google Components** library is massive and includes furniture, materials, doors, and windows. Use **Window>Components** to find components. Be as specific as possible, such as "Hermann Miller Eames Lounge Chair," to avoid sorting through too many options. Click one

component, and it will slide into the drawing exactly to scale. Then use the **Move** and **Rotate** tools to place it exactly into place. Be careful to set the component directly on the floor plate. This may take some time getting used to. (See Figures 4.10 and 4.11.) Download some furniture models and place them. If the component isn't exactly what you want, you can **Edit>Component**. Figures 4.22 through 4.24 show how you can change the scale (size) of a table.

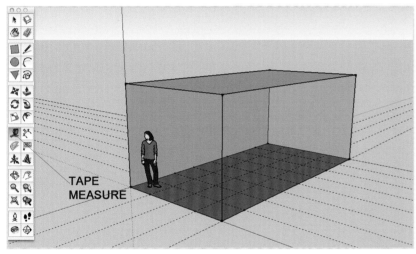

Figure 4.9 Draw guidelines using the Tape Measure tool. Select the Tape Measure tool. Click an edge that you want to measure or use as a baseline. Move the mouse a fixed distance using the distance window. In this case, use 3 feet, and then release the mouse. Press Enter. Repeat this action at 3-foot intervals in both directions at the floor plane, and you will have a guideline grid of 3-foot square. You can delete a guide with the undo button under Edit, or you can delete all guides under the Edit button.

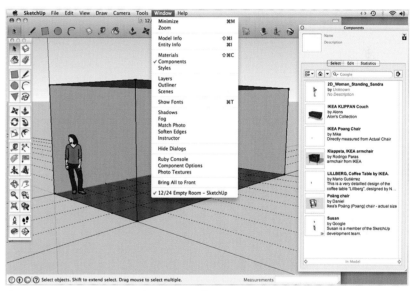

Figure 4.10a Components/Colors/Materials Menus. From the Windows menu above, drop down and select Components. Later you will do the same for Materials and Colors.

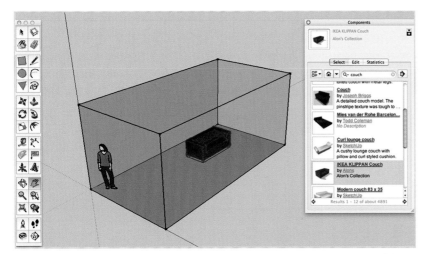

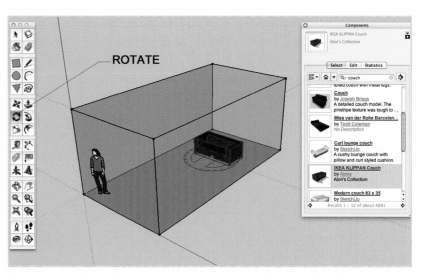

Figure 4.10b Download Components. Using the Google dialogue box at the top of the Components menu, type in specifically what type of component you want to download. You can say "Ikea couches," "Eames chairs," "Knoll tables," or others. If you just type in "chairs," you will get a large quantity of options, as Google has many options to select from. This will give you more choices. In this case, we downloaded an Ikea Klippan couch. Drag it into the image. It will appear highlighted to enable you to edit it.

Figure 4.11a Rotate. Using the Rotate command at the left, turn the item in any direction. After you start to rotate the object, you can also type in the angle of rotation, say 90 degrees, in the dialogue box.

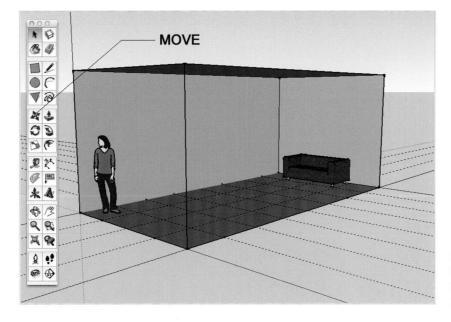

Figure 4.11b Move. After you have rotated the object, you can move it anywhere in the space. Be careful to keep it on the floor plane so it doesn't float.

Figure 4.12a Color Palette. Using the Windows pull-down menu, select Colors. You can choose from crayons or a spectrum. Then indicate the surface on the image you want to paint, and it will appear on the whole plane.

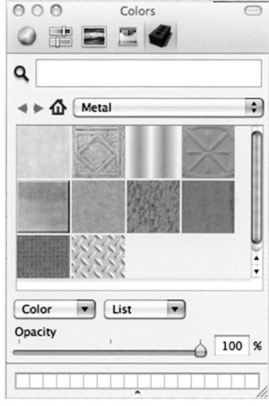

Figure 4.12b Materials Palette. Using the Windows pull-down menu, select Materials. In the dialogue box, you have a number of choices, or you can Google a specific material.

Figure 4.12c Wood Palette. Choosing the wood palette, you can select from a variety of wood colors and patterns.

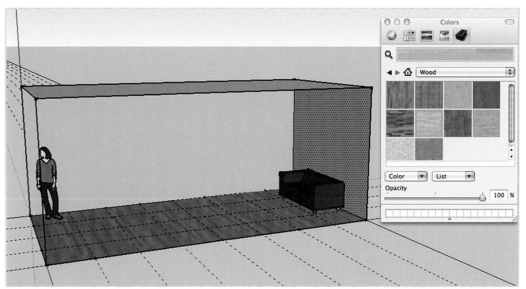

Figure 4.13 Apply Floor from Wood Palette. You can vary the opacity of the floor.

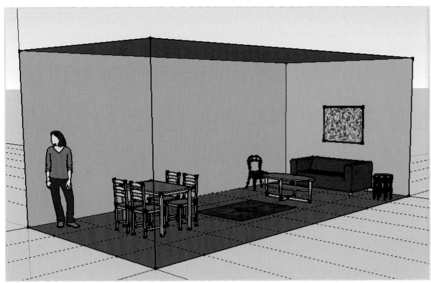

Figure 4.14 Select additional furniture components from Windows>Components and drag them to the room. We have selected the Ikea Klippan Couch, a Vejmon coffee table, a Thonet side chair, a Moroccan side table, a Persian carpet, and an Ikea Jokkmokk table (and four chairs) that come as a set. A Jackson Pollock painting hangs on the wall. You can add, delete, move, rotate, or change the components. This task is completed in a matter of minutes. You can also edit the components, which is explained later.

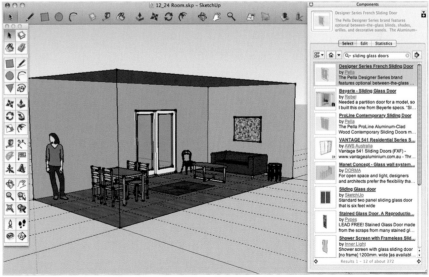

Figure 4.15 Sliding Doors. Download "sliding glass doors" from the Google dialogue box. Select Pella Designer Series French Sliding Door. Drag it to the wall.

Now you will start to use the powerful **Shadow** tool. From the **Window>Shadow** menu, set the time, date, and location of the model. The shadow will conform to these directions. Then select **View>Shadows** to turn on the shadows. **Tip**: Don't click shadows on until the end of the model, because it takes a lot of memory, and the modeling will become slow and unresponsive.

Here you can set **Dimensions** (Figure 4.17) to accurately place dimensions on your model. You can also write notes and labels with **Text**

(Figure 4.18) using the tools in the Large Tool Palette. When setting text, you can choose the smaller boxed text icon, with a leader, which will be associated with an item within the drawing. It will change locations when you orbit the drawing, so put it in toward the end when you want to take a screen shot. The larger icon, **3-D Text**, can be used for lettering within the model, such as signage.

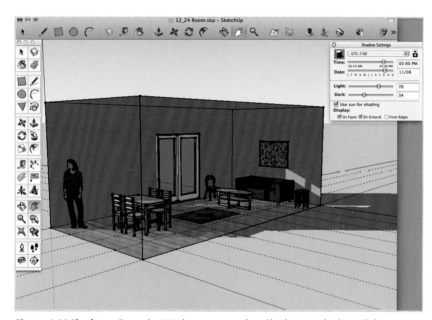

Figure 4.16 Shadows. From the Windows menu, select Shadows. A shadows dialogue box will appear, allowing you to set the time, date, lightness, and darkness of shadows, and if you want to use the sun for shading. **Tip**: From the View menu, you can toggle the Shadows on and off for quicker editing.

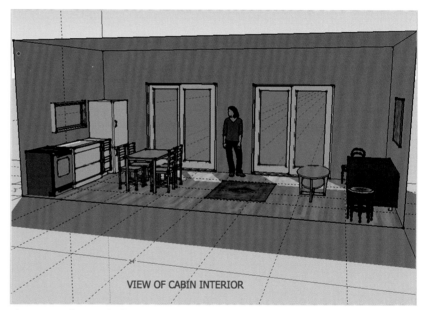

VIEW OF CABIN INTERIOR

Figure 4.17 Change Shadows. From the Windows menu, select Shadows to adjust the location, season, and time of day. Note that the title is in blue, which indicates that it is not yet fixed and can be edited with the Text tool.

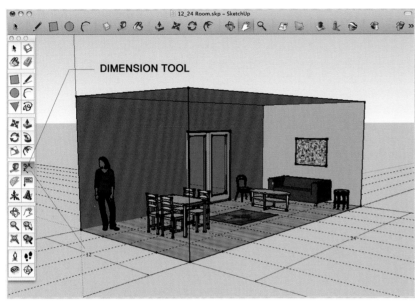

Figure 4.18 Dimensions. Use the Dimension tool to show dimensions of any part of the space or furniture. Simply click the first point, then the second point, then move the location of the dimension as you wish. In this case, we used the overall dimension of the space and then a portion of the guidelines.

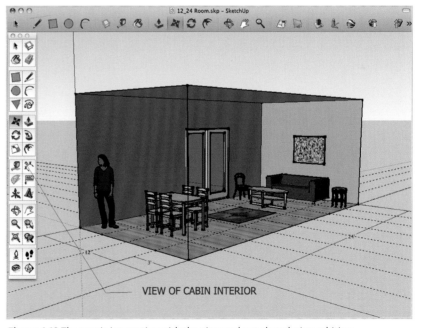

Figure 4.19 The text is interactive with the view and not clear during orbiting.

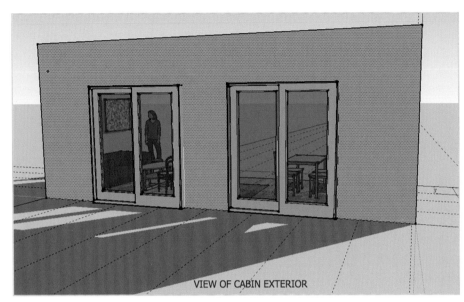

VIEW OF CABIN EXTERIOR

Figure 4.20 Copy Sliding Glass Doors-Exterior.

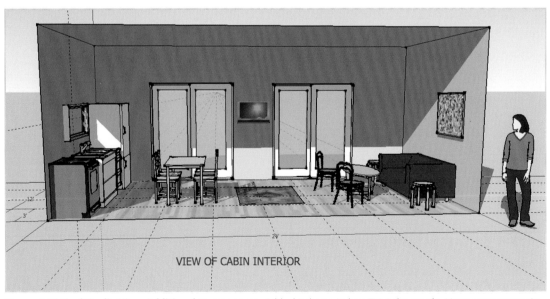

VIEW OF CABIN INTERIOR

Figure 4.21 Final Studio View, Additional Components. Add a kitchen window, TV, Aalto stools. Move components in the room. Change Shadows so the sun is in the front, not backlit.

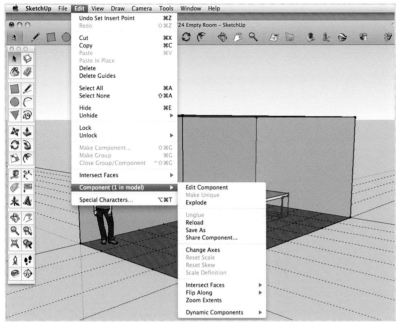

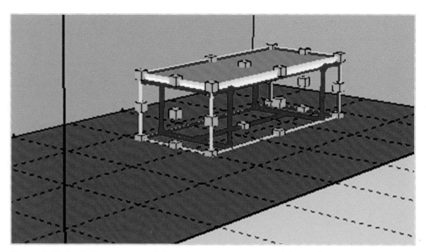

Figure 4.23 Scale Component. Select the component you wish to edit.

Figure 4.22 Edit Component. Use the Edit and Component drop-down menus to change the scale or other aspects of the component.

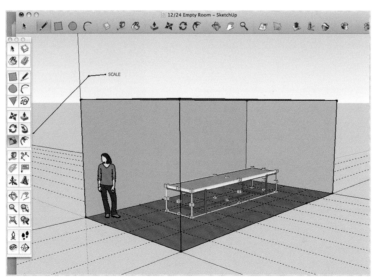

Figure 4.24 Enlarge Component with Scale Tool. In this case, we will enlarge the table. Just grab a point and drag.

Get into the habit of making groups frequently of the objects you are creating, by choosing **Select>Edit>Make Group**. This will make it easier to move them around. You can also make a library of custom furniture that you design. See how to make custom benches in Figures 4.25 and 4.26. They will be used in other projects throughout this book.

Figure 4.26 Reclining figure and seated figure.

Figure 4.25 Using the Edit>Make Group command, make a variety of rectangular shapes that can be used for benches, pillows, and backrests. Add color to the cushions by pulling down Windows>Materials>Colors. Choose whatever color you wish (we chose green), and then apply it to the cushions. Apply a wood material surface finish to the benches. Then combine them all into larger groups to form sectional seating benches. This drawing has one bench group on the left and one on the right. They can then be copied and pasted into other drawings. You can also use the Edit>Flip command for components to give a mirrored image. Download figures from the Components menu.

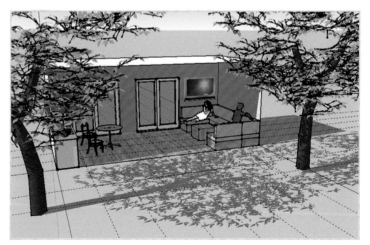

Figure 4.27 Trees. To provide some context, select Trees from the Components menu. Find one or two that you like, and download them to the studio view. Then select Window>Shadows and select the time of day for the best configuration.

Download some trees and turn on the **View>Shadow** button. We have left the exterior walls off to better view the interior.

Now we will expand this **Studio** model to add a bedroom/bathroom (BR/BA) suite. Sketch it out first with a freehand bubble diagram, and then draw a floor plan. (See Figures 4.28 to 4.30.) Add landscaping and view this house from the street and from the backyard. (See Figures 4.31 and 4.32.) In this simple model, you have learned to use several very important tools.

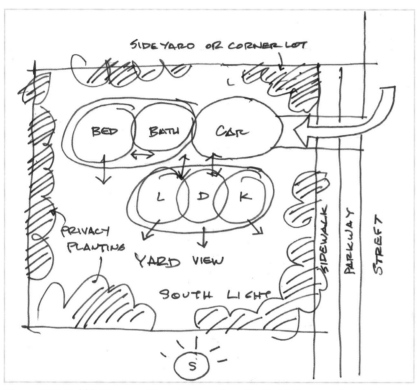

Figure 4.28a Bubble Diagram. Now step away from the SketchUp concept sketches. It's time to think through what you want from this project and how you want to place it on the site. Nothing is quicker than Bubble Diagrams to sketch out your alternatives. Freehand, and without the need for scale or accuracy, you can arrive at the diagram for your project. Your clients have decided that they want a bedroom/bathroom suite added to the studio so they can live in it year-round. The street and pedestrian access are shown on the right of the drawing.

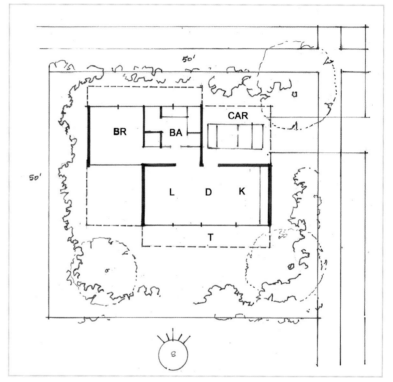

Figure 4.28b Site Plan. Trying and discarding different site plans, we arrive at one that satisfies various needs: a master BR/BA suite that includes separate functions, southern sunlight, offstreet parking under a carport, and landscaping for privacy. The living/dining/kitchen (LD/K) are left open as a great room. There is an open terrace (T) fronting on the south garden. The footprint is a compact 566 square feet net interior area. This shows how the freehand drawing can help inform the digital concept model we are making.

Figure 4.29 House with One Bedroom and One Bathroom. We will now add onto the SketchUp model of the studio to complete the vision of a small one-bedroom house of 566 square feet. (Additional house planning will follow in Part III.)

Figure 4.30a Bedroom/Bathroom Suite. This illustration of a bedroom/bathroom suite shows the adjacency of bedroom to bathroom. In the bathroom, it's important to separate the water closet from the bathing area, so two people can share the bathroom with privacy. It's also important to provide a washer/dryer close to the plumbing and the clothes closets. From the Components menu, download a soaking tub, a vanity/lavatory, a water closet, and a combined European-style washer/dryer.

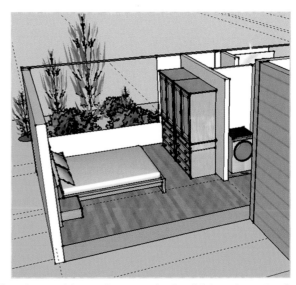

Figure 4.30b Bedroom with Armoires. Download prefabricated armoires from the Components menu for clothes storage. They have drawers as well as hanging space.

Figure 4.31 View from Street with Carport. Download a compact Smart Car to nestle under the carport roof. A Toyota Prius is parked in the street.

Figure 4.32 View from the Yard. Part of the exterior cladding is not shown so that interior details can be seen. Download tall trees and low shrubs to form the yard. Many landscape elements can be downloaded from Google's menu.

Tools Used in This Chapter

1. Orbit and pan for viewing from different angles
2. Zoom to go in and out
3. Draw line, rectangle, circle
4. Push/pull or extrude shapes to make them 3D
5. Tape measure to measure or draw guidelines
6. Downloading components and materials
7. Rotating objects
8. Moving objects
9. Text for writing and titling
10. Dimensions to show size
11. Scale for changing size of objects

Background

The program SketchUp debuted in 2000, nearly 20 years after Auto-CAD. By then, AutoCAD was well developed and used by nearly every design professional in the U.S. market. It remains an excellent tool for 2D drawings, particularly working drawings or construction documents. Designers, however, were seeking a tool that they could use directly in 3D—something readily accessible, affordable (free), and very user friendly. SketchUp's tag line was originally "3D for everyone." It does a great job of creating quick 3D models that can be viewed instantly from any number of angles. (Its finishes, however, may not always be exactly to scale and a little cartoony.) SketchUp also allows the designer to study the effects of sun and shadows. Google acquired SketchUp in 2006 and it now provides a huge library, thousands of components, furniture, landscape, people, and cars, which can be downloaded into the SketchUp models. In addition, many manufacturers now offer their products in SketchUp format for use with 3D models through the Google Warehouse.

KEY TERMS

Menu: The horizontal bar across the top of the SketchUp screen that lists 21 tools and actions to use on models

Large tool menu: Under View>Palette>Large Tool Palette, you can access a larger menu of 32 items at the left of the screen.

Orbit: A tool that allows you to "fly around" to different viewpoints within your model

Tools: The specific items shown on the SketchUp menu that allow you to work on your models

Floor plate: Flat plane indicating the extent of the floor plan. In SketchUp, this plate can be extruded into a 3D plate, say 6 to 12 inches thick. Then made into a group so it can be moved.

EXERCISES AND PRACTICE

1. Try placing exterior walls, doors, and windows on this model.
2. Practice using different sized rectangles and extruded solids.
3. Arrange them on the site in different relationships to each other.

(See Pappageorge Haymes's private residence in **Chapter 12**, Single-Family Homes, for an example of the development of a SketchUp model.)

CHAPTER 5

Photoshop Techniques

Objectives

- Add color quickly to hand sketches.
- Learn how to collage designs into existing sites.
- Transform the size and perspective of images to match existing site photos.
- Add entourages of people, streetscapes, cars, and trees to modeled images.
- Change color schemes quickly.
- Learn how to convert SketchUp files to Photoshop files for combining and editing.
- Learn how SketchUp views can be saved as jpegs and converted to Adobe Photoshop, where they can be merged with other images.
- Learn a variety of different techniques that can be used to edit combined files from different platforms.

Overview

Although it is not possible to describe all of the techniques contained in Photoshop in this book, **Chapter 5** shows the basic activities that are most useful for interior designers and architects. Photoshop is an extremely powerful program, possessing multiple tools and variations. Interior designers, photographers, publishers, and architects use it extensively. Photoshop was released for Macintosh exclusively in 1990, and it has quickly become the industry standard for digital image editing.[1]

Getting Started with Photoshop

You may have heard that Photoshop is a program for photographers, to retouch photos or enhance their color, contrast, and brightness. This is true, but many of these adjustments can now be made in iPhoto. Photoshop is so much more. For architects and designers, it's a way to provide context for your projects, for example, through different color schemes or different outdoor views. And it's a way to import images for collage.

To start using Photoshop, first you must set up the sheet. Although you can format large sheets, you can also set up templates for different sizes. We will start with an $8\frac{1}{2}$-by-11-inch sheet, so that it can be printed on a home printer. As shown in Figure 5.1, choose inches from the dialogue box. The resolution is entirely dependent on the final output you intend. For images to be shown only on screens, such as slideshows,

---

1. http://en.wikipedia.org/wiki/Adobe_Photoshop#Early_history

PowerPoints, or for emailing, a resolution of 72 pixels per inch is standard. Print documents require 200 to 300 dots per inch if they are printed at the same size as their original. Larger images require a greater amount of disc storage space, so be frugal.

You should save some folders for images that you know you may use in the future, such as people, cars, trees, urban buildings, furniture, and landscapes. As you add images to these folders (or albums in Photoshop), you can easily find them when you need them for a presentation.

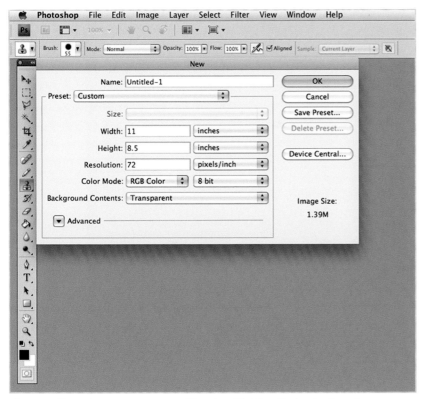

Figure 5.1 Sheet Setup. To start a new file, select File>New. Under the drop-down Menu>Image>Image Size, you can set the size as you wish. For screen viewing, 8½ by 11 inches at 72 pixels per inch is sufficient. For printing, set the image size you will print at with a resolution of 300 dots per inch.

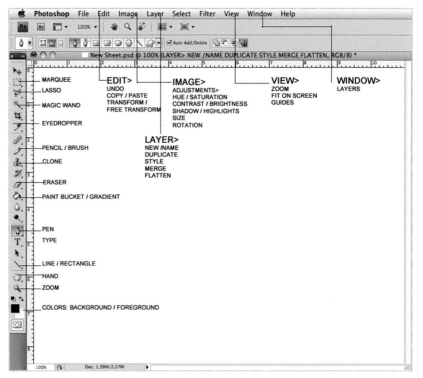

Figure 5.2 Startup Menus and Tools. This is a map of the most useful menus and tools in Photoshop for designers. The main menu is across the top and the toolbar is to the left.

The startup page for Photoshop identifies 37 different basic commands (explained in the text), and many of them have subcommands. It is not possible to go into detail for all of those commands here, but we can give examples of where basic commands are located and encourage you to explore within them.

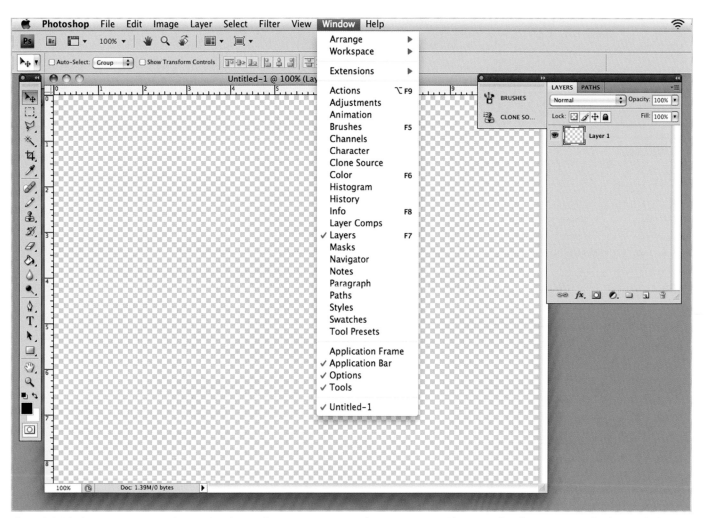

Figure 5.3 Windows Menu›Layers. By opening the Windows Menu at top, you have access to a wide range of toolbars. Importantly, these include Arrange Workspace (for toggling between Cascade and Tiles), Layers, Color, Text/Notes/Paragraphs (for typing), Options, and Tools. Press them to see what appears. Layers will become increasingly important. **Tip:** The eyeball icon next to the Layer name is for making certain layers invisible if you don't want to see them.

Now you can begin to use some of the tools. The most important of these is Layers. Go to **Windows>Layers** for the layer palette. First, you can double-click the base image to unlock it, so you can work on it. Then go to **Layer>New** and open a New Layer. Name it for its function, such as Pencil, Background Color, or anything you might want separate from the original image. Changing size through **Transform** should also be held on a separate layer. (This will be described in more detail in subsequent chapters.) Text Blocks usually open a new layer for each block, and then you can name it by what it writes. Using multiple layers tends to increase the disc space used. Using the layer menu, at certain points, you may want to merge some of the layers or flatten them to save disc space. This is an option in the Layer command. Also note that the **Document Size** is on the bottom length of the image (in this case, 1.39 MB), shown in Figure 5.4a. Keep an eye on this as you add information and layers.

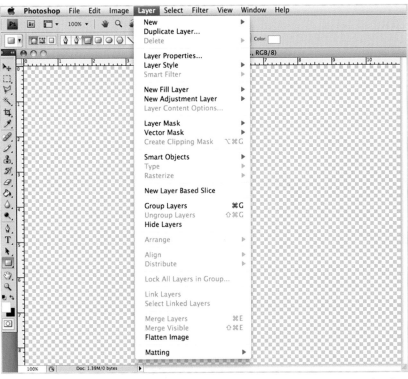

Figure 5.4a Layer. Layer is one of the most powerful tools in Photoshop. You can develop multiple images, partially delete areas, combine layers, and influence colors from one layer to the next. In short, you can work on one layer without disturbing the others. (Examples will be shown.) You can also edit or duplicate layers. In the Layers window, you will notice a dialogue box defaulting to Normal. (Later you will see how setting it to Multiply will allow lines to show through solid layers.)

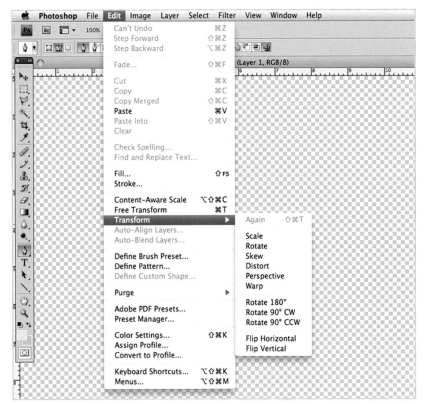

Figure 5.4b Edit>Transform>Perspective. You can adjust the image scale, resolution, contrast, and brightness, as well as its color hues, saturation, and value. You can also skew it into any perspective view.

You will frequently want to produce a simple line drawing and then change its background. To do this, you must first isolate the line work from the white background. There are different ways to do this. For the image shown in this chapter, we chose St. Malo, a French historical monument in Brittany. The church was built on the ruins of previous ancient temples and churches over more than twenty centuries. Spending time there, particularly at dusk, dawn, and night, one is impressed and moved by the changing color of the atmosphere produced through the damp air. With Photoshop, you can record and change many different moods.

Figure 5.5a Line Drawing of St. Malo Walls, Brittany, France. This drawing was made on site with India ink on white Strathmore Bristol, then scanned into Photoshop.

1. Choose the **magic wand** tool and select within the line area. Then select the inverse and press delete. Only the lines will remain. You may miss some spaces, so do it again until it is clean.

2. Choose **Select>Color Range** and place the eye dropper on the white background. (See Figure 5.5b.) When the white is selected, click delete and eliminate it, leaving a transparent background.

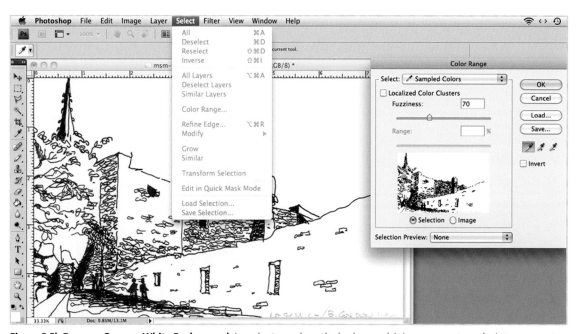

Figure 5.5b Remove Opaque White Background. In order to work on the background, it is necessary to make it transparent. This is easily achieved by choosing Select>Color Range>Dialogue Box. The dialogue box shows the eye dropper tool, which can be clicked on the white background area to select it. (**Tip**: Set the fuzziness slider low to select the pixels that are closest in color to your selection.) Click OK on the dialogue box. Then click Delete and *voila*! All of the pixels with that color, namely the entire background area, disappears. Then draw down from the Select>Deselect Menu, and the area will be deselected. This can be used on any color.

3. You can fill the background with any color you like or place an image on another layer, such as a distant landscape or other buildings. Use the **Color Select** tool in the lower left-hand corner.

4. You can also use a **Gradient Fill**, which is nestled in the **Paint Bucket** icon to show a color dissolving from darker to lighter. It will ask you to draw a line from top to bottom or left to right to show the gradient. Play with this a little to see how it works.

5. If you have added another image on a separate layer, use **Edit>Transform**. You can change it on that separate layer without affecting the other layers. That is, you can change the size, rotate it, distort it, correct the perspective, and other useful changes. If you want to use the eraser tool on one of your images, or part of your image, be sure you have placed it on a separate layer so you can erase it without affecting the other parts of the image.

Figure 5.5c Now you have a line drawing with a transparent background, which can be colored by adding background and foreground layers.

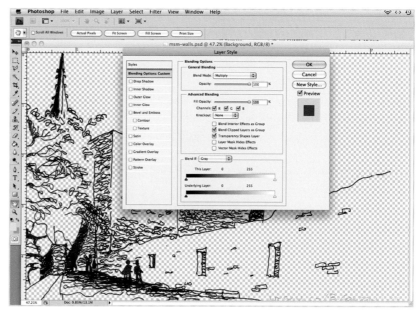

Figure 5.6 Blending Options. Layer>Layer Style>Blending Options>Blend Mode>Multiply will allow you to use overlay layers where the lines show through the painted layer.

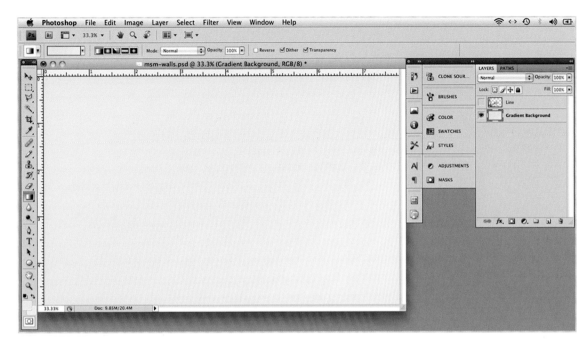

Figure 5.7a Gradient Layer. Add a new Layer; call it Gradient Background.

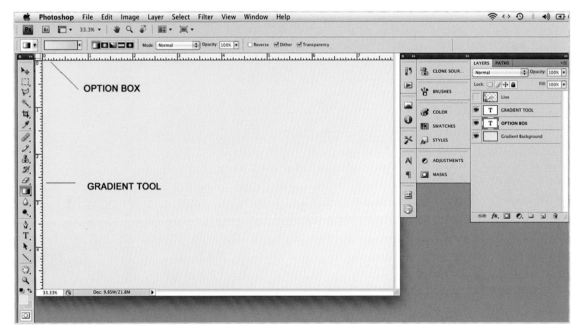

Figure 5.7b Gradient Tool. It is nestled within the Paint Bucket tool at left. (**Tip**: This icon can be easily mistaken for the rectangle icon, so be careful. This will open a dialogue box in the Options Window above, allowing you to adjust the colors and the type of gradient you want. Then, from the boxes to the right, choose Linear Gradient, the first box. This will allow you to draw a pen line across the selected image. The gradation will appear instantly. Try different lines for different gradients.)

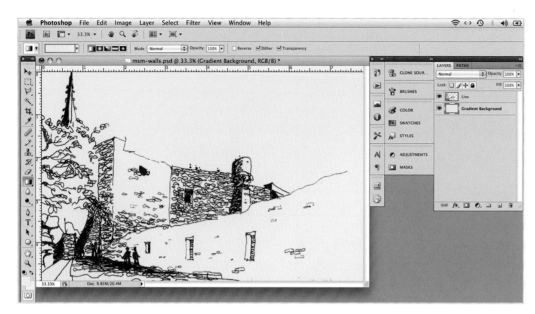

Figure 5.7c Open the Line Layer. See the whole drawing.

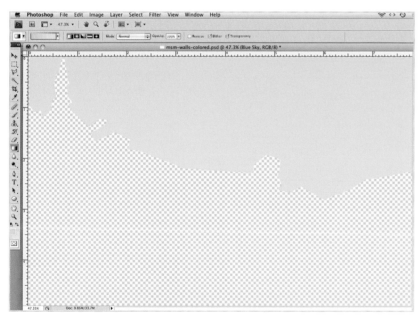

Figure 5.8 Try a Gradient Sky to Show a Sunset or Sunrise. Here you can also place a sky photo from your own library.

Figure 5.9 If you want the line work to show through a color area, choose Layer>Layer Style>Blending Options>Multiply.

Basic Tools for Photoshop

In future chapters, we explore the use of the drop-down menu items, from the top of the screen, as well as the basic tools nestled within the icons:

1. **Layers**. One of the great strengths of Photoshop is that it can be separated into layers so that different images can be worked on at the same time and merged into one image.
2. **Edit> Cut, Copy, Paste, Undo** and other familiar functions are found here. Image Adjustments are also found here.
3. **Image Adjustments**. You can adjust the image size, resolution, contrast, and brightness, as well as its color hues, saturation, and value.
4. **Transform**. Under **Edit**, there is a very useful tool called **Transform**, which allows you to scale, skew, warp, or correct perspective.
5. **Filters**. Various filters are also used to change the character of the line work and images, giving effects ranging from hand drawing to watercolor to brushstrokes to pixelation.
6. **Viewing> Zooms, Rulers, Guides**

We also describe some of the basic tools in Photoshop from the toolbar menu, located at the left:

1. Pencil tool and line size
2. Brush
3. Measuring and navigation
4. Selection, marquee, rectangular, and lasso
5. Eye dropper
6. Magic wand
7. Cropping
8. Slicing
9. Moving
10. Rotating
11. Eraser
12. Paint bucket and gradient fill
13. Typing
14. Retouching (clone tool) and brush size
15. Eye dropper
16. Paint bucket (areas of color)
17. Gradient backgrounds

Photoshop is used in many of the images shown in the Art Gallery sections in this book. After modeling in SketchUp or other programs, it's not uncommon to save images as "screenshots" and open them in Photoshop for enhancement and editing. When you find an image from SketchUp or any other source, you can save it by taking a screenshot. Press (command + shift + 4) on Mac to allow you to select an area on the screen and take a snapshot. It will be saved as a png file, and you can open it up in Photoshop and save as a jpeg.

KEY TERMS

Layer: A tool in Photoshop that allows different images to be saved in the same file without affecting each other, so they can be edited separately

Collage: Pasting different images on layers in Photoshop, similar to paper collages

Magic wand: A selection tool in Photoshop that "magically" selects irregular areas

Screenshots: When you find an image on screen, you can save just that image by taking a screenshot of it.

Paint bucket: A tool that allows spreading large areas of color on Photoshop layers, like tipping a paint can sideways

Gradient: Similar to Paint Bucket, but it can dissolve one color into another

Transform: Change of the state of an image in one layer without affecting the whole image

EXERCISES AND PRACTICE

1. Take several digital photos and save them in folders to organize them. In iPhoto, you can save them in albums without adding any storage to your disc.
2. Select a basic image and try different backgrounds, landscapes, and buildings.
3. Choose an interior view with large windows, preferably a corner, and select the window areas and delete them. Try different exterior views through these windows.
4. Depending on the exterior colors, change the color scheme of the interior to harmonize with the exterior view.
5. Place people in your views, whether they are standing outside or sitting down inside. People should be kept on separate layers, where they can be transformed in size, used as photos, or filled with shading or color, and the opacity of the fill can be adjusted. **Tip**: You can even create line outlines of the figures by using **Filter>Stylize>Find Edges**. That way the style of people you use will conform to the style of your drawing. It's important to keep people relatively realistic, and certainly in scale, but they shouldn't dominate the interior view you are showing.

Mixed Media: Integrating Techniques

Objectives

- Learn how to combine the various graphic techniques that you have learned in previous chapters, freehand and digital, for developing a design presentation.
- Understand how your rendering choices affect the impact your design will have on the client.

Overview

It may be difficult to decide which technique to use when starting a design. Part of it depends on what you hope to achieve and how much time you have to do it. Another part depends on what you think your client's expectations may be. It's also a matter of personal work style choices. In **Chapter 6**, we approach the problem by starting first from hand drawing, and then using digital modeling to develop and investigate the design. We will place these freehand drawings and models into Photoshop for presentation purposes. Then we will reverse the order and experiment with using the digital model as a basis for hand drawing. (Note that AutoCAD drawings can also be imported into SketchUp and saved to Photoshop files. We mention this only for information since we are not concentrating on AutoCAD in this book.)

The Studio to Home Project

This is where the work becomes interesting. It's a personal creative choice how to start a drawing. The challenges for the current generation of designers may be that there are too many choices to begin with, but there are also numerous possibilities. In this case, let's start with a hand drawing of the studio from **Chapter 4**. Draw a cross section. You can trace the SketchUp model for dimensions or draft it by hand. Tracing over the freehand section, you can study different roof possibilities: flat roof, shed roof, or gable roof. Having settled on the gable roof, extend the space forward as a one-point perspective. This view shows the interior furnishings as well as the relationship of indoors to out. Upstairs, with access by a ladder, you can fit a sleeping loft, guest room, office, or storage.

Now let's look at the exterior of the studio. Because we have modeled the studio in SketchUp, we can explore different views. Select the ones you like best and trace over them to establish a freehand style of presentation. Here a sheet of paper was placed over the model, tracing the model to provide color and texture. Save these two images combined as a single jpeg image. Open the image with Photoshop, and you can use your own pictures from the folder you've saved for People. If you don't find an image you like, search the Internet for images of people that you may want to use in your photo rendering. Of course, you must obtain the necessary permission from anyone whose image you may use.

Figure 6.2b shows a drawing combining a SketchUp model, freehand tracing, and a Photoshop enhancement, including importing people for the image. You can do this in any order or any combination you wish. The next figure shows the same sketch with the background removed for a simpler presentation.

Note: Start with the studio we developed in **Chapter 4**. Remember, you can think of this as an addition to a home for a guest room or as a freestanding art studio on the home site. The purpose of this exercise is to study the different commands and how they can be mixed with freehand drawing and rendering in the context of an actual building.

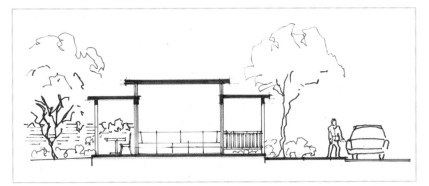

Figure 6.1a Section A. Flat Roof. Using hand drafting and quick freehand sketching, trace over SketchUp drawings from **Chapter 4** to explore different roof sections. Roof in main room is 10 feet high, and porches are at 8-foot ceiling height. There is an entry porch facing the street and a terrace porch facing the yard.

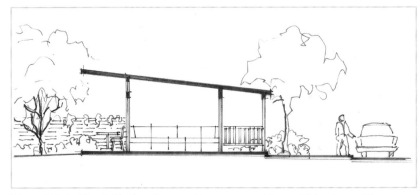

Figure 6.1b Section B. Shed roof over entire structure, rising up higher toward the yard (south).

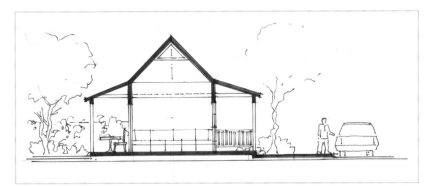

Figure 6.1c Section C. Set a gable roof at a 45-degree angle from the 10-foot wall height. Then drop to 8 feet high for the mezzanine(s), which can be accessed by attic ladder. This allows standup height in the attic, so that it can be used for extra sleeping spaces.

Figure 6.1d Pictorial Section D. Again, tracing over the SketchUp drawing, extend the sectional view into a perspective. This type of view, sometimes called a section/perspective, helps describe what is actually happening in a room. This is a favorite view for many clients, who appreciate the help in visualizing the space. You can see the foreground in 3D, showing the furniture, lighting, and attic space.

Figure 6.2a Street View, Overlay Drawing. Sometimes freehand drawing is employed before making a SketchUp view, but here it is traced over the SketchUp image. It is a black ink line drawing over the SketchUp image.

Figure 6.2b People in Front of House. Search the Internet for Entourage downloads for Photoshop. They are numerous. Select a group of people and copy them to the front of the house to add some context.

Figure 6.2c Street View, Line Drawing. Here is the same drawing separated from the SketchUp image. From this stage, you can also make a color rendering.

Figure 6.3a Yard View, Overlay Drawing. This is a view from the yard sketched over the SketchUp image.

Figure 6.3b Yard View, Line Drawing. The same view, with just the line drawing shown. **Note**: Now proceed to the one-bedroom house that we developed from adding on to the studio in **Chapter 4**.

Figure 6.4a Street View. This is a line drawing traced over the SketchUp image of the one-bedroom house. This shows the carport and pedestrian entry. Notice that we have added high windows facing the street on the tracing. This is a colorful rendering in itself, but you can also print out the line drawing on bond paper and use markers and colored pencils. Although it is not a finished drawing, notice that we have blended a SketchUp image, Photoshop, a line drawing, and a download of people in front to get a feeling for the design.

Figure 6.4b Street View, Line Drawing. Here is the same drawing separated from the SketchUp image. From this stage, you can also make a color rendering.

Following is a series of simple exterior sketches made from SketchUp models: a backyard view, a street view, and a garden. Study the different views of the model and select those that best describe the project. This is one of the great aspects of SketchUp. Place a sheet of tracing paper over the SketchUp models you like best and trace them. Then you can separate them, so you can look at them as line drawings without color. The type of presentation you use is entirely up to you and the way you want it to look for your client. Remembering the idea we advanced earlier, you may prefer to show clients freehand drawings so they feel they can participate in the design, or you may wish to present it as more finished with digital imagery.

Figure 6.5a Garden View from South. This is also a line drawing traced over the SketchUp image of the one-bedroom house. This image shows the arrangement of trees and shrubs. By turning on the Shadow (View>Shadow), you can see how the sun affects the landscape and yard at any time of day, in any season.

Figure 6.5b Garden View, Line Drawing. Here is the same drawing separated from the SketchUp image. From this stage, you can also make a color rendering.

In Figures 6.6a–c, this rendering of a townhouse development is a collage made from site photographs and a cutout rendering of the house. This is old school style. No digital technique was used, but the drawing was collaged onto a site photo. The drawing is freehand over a constructed perspective, rendered with markers and colored pencils.

Figure 6.6a Townhouse Rendering. Hand-rendered perspective in marker and colored pencils.

Figure 6.6b Townhouses, Front Elevation. View of townhouses from street. Hand rendered and collaged to photo.

Figure 6.6c Townhouses, Front. Showing adjoining property. Old school style, made with drawing glued over photograph. The same image could be made more easily today with Photoshop.

For this apartment building in the Oakland Hills (Figures 6.7a–c), we will use the **Edit>Transform** tool in Photoshop. This is a way to see how your project fits in the context of the site and adjoining structures. First, take a series of good digital images and select one that best shows your project. Use the **Select>Lasso** tool to remove any existing structures you may not want. The Lasso tool is a selection tool that allows selection of irregular objects, point by point, instead of using the conventional rectangle. It also allows oval, polygonal, and magnetic selections. Try it and then hit delete to delete selections. After deleting the unwanted areas, make a freehand sketch of your proposed design. Scan it and import it to Photoshop on a new Layer, which you can call Sketch. Now you can **Edit>Free Transform** to get it just the size you want. The result is a quick sketch of the proposed building superimposed on the existing site and next to the adjoining property. You can try several different concepts quickly using this technique.

Figure 6.7a Hillside House Site, Oakland Hills. The area deleted is to prepare it for a Layer beneath with house sketches.

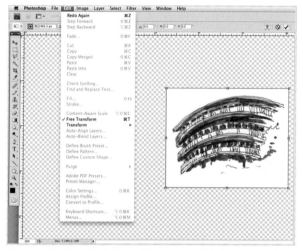

Figure 6.7b Skew, Rotation of the Image. This is particularly useful when bringing in images on new layers so they conform to the base image.

Figure 6.7c Hillside House Collage. Showing how a quick sketch of the massing can be collaged on a layer to see how it will look. The amount of detail on the sketch can vary.

View Pavilion

Now we're going to study how a simple, open pavilion fits into, and is affected by, its environment. (See Figures 6.8–6.10.) We will also explore several new Photoshop tools in the process. The pavilion is shown with walls and windows hidden in SketchUp (**Edit>Hide**). This allows us to peer into the interior and still see the exterior views. It's not meant to be realistic, but rather as an analytical tool. Turn off the **View>Shadows** tool where shadows conflict with the image you're showing. The first model used a SketchUp component for a

hilly landscape. View it first in plan and then as an open view through the columns. Now look at some views from the yard side and gradually zoom in until you're in the interior. In Figure 6.8c, use the Lasso tool to select and then delete the view between the columns. Now you can experiment with different view panoramas. You can view the same pavilion sited in Lake Merritt, in Oakland, California, on the Pacific coast in Monterey, California, or travel to Paris where you can see Notre Dame or the Eiffel Tower at night. If you can't actually travel there, you can certainly imagine it.

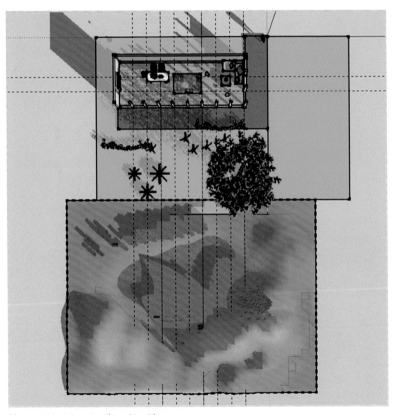

Figure 6.8a View Pavilion Site Plan.

Figure 6.8b View Pavilion Floor Plan.

Figure 6.8c Hill Panorama. Viewed through pavilion.

Figure 6.8d Interior View. Hill background for interior.

Figure 6.8e Yard View.

Figure 6.9a Interior with Yard.
No Background.

**Figure 6.9b Remove
Window Areas.** Allowing
views of different contexts.
Remove window areas with
Select>Color Range>Delete,
as before.

Figure 6.10a Lake Merritt View.

Figure 6.10b San Francisco Bay View.

Figure 6.10c Notre Dame View, Paris.

Figure 6.10d Eiffel Tower at Night.

Digital modeling: Using computer imaging to create basic 3D models

Edit›Transform: Editing a layer in Photoshop to adjust size and shape

Pavilion: A separate structure from a home that can be used for parties or festivals

Edit›Hide: A tool whereby you can hide elements in SketchUp so you can see through them. Then you can unhide them without redrawing.

View›Shadows: A button to turn off the shadows in an image. This speeds up the time of use, as well as provides blank planes for interior lighting.

Filter›Render›Lighting Effect: The tool for adding lighting to a Photoshop image

Intensity: The brightness of a light

Focus: The range over which a light is spread on a surface

Reflective properties: The amount of reflection is based on the smoothness of a surface.

Ambience: The area in a room or space that is not lighted. This is important to show the contrast with the lighting so that a room is not too dark or too light.

1. Find several rooms to photograph, and also sketch them freehand.
2. Find the horizon line and vanishing points on your photographs and compare them to your sketches.
3. Choose the best sketches, and render them by hand with markers and colored pencils.
4. Open the photos in Photoshop and adjust the images by using the Image›Contrast, brightness tool.
5. Change colors on these images with color adjustments.
6. Open some of these images in Photoshop and try using Filters for special effects. Turn your photos into watercolors, for example.

ART GALLERY

Now we're going to turn this pavilion into a lively nightspot, an art gallery, where we can import shadow people and study lighting effects in Photoshop. Look at three somewhat different views from the street, for different heights. (The walls and front have been removed to view the interior). Moving closer in to see the artwork, we will now try the **Filter>Render>Lighting Effect** tool. This will give you a sense of lighting certain areas in the scene. It won't be entirely realistic, but at least it shows how lighting can affect an interior space. Sometimes you may want to turn the View>Shadow tool off to make this clearer. The dialogue box for lighting effects allows several different adjustments, shown in Figure G6.1f, as follows:

- Lighting Styles>Spotlights, flood lights, triple lights, and others
- It will allow you to *switch* the lights on and off.
- The *intensity* can go from negative to full.
- The *focus* of the area can be adjusted from narrow to wide.
- *Reflective properties* of objects can be matte or shiny.
- And very importantly, the *ambience* must be adjusted. Otherwise, the room will appear either too dark or too light.

It takes some time playing with this tool to get it the way you want it, but it's worth the trouble. Lighting a room is extremely important in interior design. This will complete the tour of lighting in Photoshop for now, but this topic will reappear in subsequent chapters for lighting interior rooms by various types of lamps and lights.

Figure G6.1b Art Gallery, View from Street.

Figure G6.1a Art Gallery, Bird's-eye View. Through Windows>Components, you can load trees, cars, paintings, spotlighting, and people.

Figure G6.1c Art Gallery, Sidewalk View, Storefront. Notice that the people we downloaded cast their own shadows. Shadows can also be added manually when necessary. Copy the figure to a new Layer, Rotate it flat, (away from the light), then Image>Adjust>Darken it. Then you can Select>Modify>Feather for the edges.

Figure G6.1d Art Gallery, Closeup showing Picasso's *Guernica*, a Van Gogh, and Matisse paintings with natural lighting.

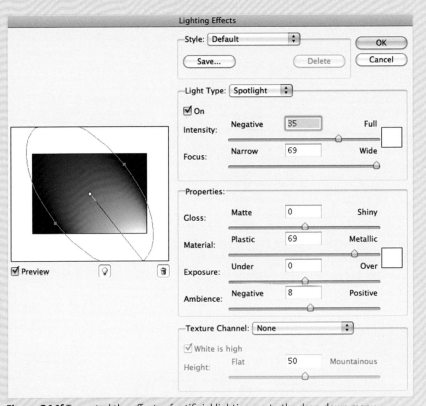

Figure G6.1f To control the effects of artificial lighting, go to the drop-down menu Filters>Rendering >Lighting Effects, which opens a dialogue box for adjustments.

Figure G6.1e Art Gallery, Same Closeup with Lighting Effects added. To show the effects of artificial lighting, go to the drop-down menu Filters>Rendering>Lighting Effects, which opens a dialogue box for adjustments. (See Figure G6.1f.)

Residential Design with Integrated Media

Part III will take you through the design and rendering of different kinds of residential projects.

You will see how the foyer (**Chapter 7**) is an important first step into the dwelling unit. The great room (**Chapter 8**) is also an important space. Other important single rooms include the kitchen (**Chapter 9**) and the bathroom (**Chapter 10**). You will be introduced to compact size rooms and to larger luxury suites. Rooms are based on the 12-by-12-foot module for planning purposes, but the furniture arrangements are based on practical, everyday functional requirements.

After the room studies, you will learn about adjacencies, the study of which rooms should be located adjoining each other (**Chapter 11**). You will use the Copy and Paste tools from SketchUp to try different combinations. Great rooms can be divided into private spaces for various uses. In Photoshop, we will use the Filter>Render>Lighting Effect tool to illuminate these spaces.

All of the examples in these chapters were put together to show how they could be used for different housing types appropriate to their sites (**Chapters 12 and 13**).

CHAPTER 7

The Foyer: Entering the Home and Connecting the Elements

Objectives

- Show the functions and sizes of various types of foyers and their location in the home.
- Compare home foyers to apartment foyers.
- Use photography and different SketchUp and drawing tools to show the functions of the various types of foyers.
- Learn how to use the Wacom digital pen in drawings.

First Impressions and Why They Matter

"Make a good first impression" is the common advice given for meeting new people. It is recognized that first impressions can be lasting, even though they may actually last no more than a few seconds. This is also true of buildings. This is why the foyer, or reception area—even if it is very small—can be a critical first step in the design of any type of building.

A basic foyer can be a very small space in a residence, where it can serve the purpose of a brief transition area before entering the rest of the apartment. It is still important to include basic needs of entry, such as a:

- Place to hang coats
- Place to drop keys
- Carpet to wipe and/or remove shoes
- Freshen-up mirror
- Space to display artwork or family photos

Medium-sized foyers can include more luxurious comforts, such as a:

- Bench for seating
- Closet
- Full-length mirror

A full-sized foyer can even include a small, extra flexible-space room, such as a den, home office, or a guest room. You can also provide a lavatory, or powder room.

Tip: Use the aforementioned items in a client questionnaire before design to determine what should be included in the foyer. The benefits of this modest space can far outweigh its cost. Remember, even a small foyer can make an apartment appear much larger than it actually is and keep clutter out of the main rooms.

Modules

Throughout Part III, we use a 12-by-12-foot module for planning individual spaces. This is for several reasons:

1. It is a convenient size and scale for many of the functions in a home, such as sitting, dining, preparing food, sleeping, bathing, and toileting.
2. It corresponds to an economical and common structural system for residential building.
3. It is useful for comparing one plan against another, using the same areas.
4. There is flexibility. The 12-foot module can be doubled, making it 24 feet. Even 30 feet is common in many apartment buildings. We wanted to settle on one size.
5. This dimension could vary depending on the location of the project. In Paris, for example, where space is limited, 10 feet (3 meters) is more common. In a suburban area, there might be larger planning areas, say 14 to 16 feet.

Although the 12-foot module is often used for prefabricated, or modular, housing, it is not the intention for using the module in this book. The housing unit itself is only a fraction of the residential unit budget—in some cases less than half. Much of the cost of housing is taken up by land cost, foundations, underground water, sewers, electricity, and site preparation. Local conditions will dictate whether it is more economical to prefabricate or build on-site. The use of the module here is intended purely for planning purposes.

Photographic Surveys

As in other categories in this book, we recommend taking digital photos of interiors and exteriors of foyers to better understand their functions. For this purpose, we are introducing a new tool, the digital pen. It works freehand and acts much like a standard pen. Wacom manufactures several grades and sizes. They have good customer service for advice on what type of digital pen to buy and how to use it. Open your photos in Photoshop to make notes directly on your images.

Figure 7.1 The Wacom digital pen and tablet is an indispensable device for those who wish to sketch digitally or make notes on photos.

Figure 7.2a Front Exterior Entry, Single-Family House. Consider the exterior entry to buildings to get a sense of the design context you will use for interior foyers.

Figure 7.2b Notes made on the Front Entry slide, showing positive and negative aspects of the entry, the shelter of the canopy, and accessibility issues of the stairs.

Figure 7.3 House with Side Entry, Allowing Bay Window Front. Foyer is set back.

Figure 7.4 Apartment Building Entry with Curved Driveway. There may also be a doorman or communication phone for security. The interior foyer will be accessed by a corridor.

Figure 7.5 Apartment Building Entry on Street. Heavy doors for security. These are usually accessed by speaker phone.

Figure 7.6 Entry for Mixed-Use Building. Retail at ground floor, apartments above.

Figure 7.7 Entry for Glass Tower by Mies Van Der Rohe, 860–880 N. Lake Shore Drive, Chicago. Although glass towers are an elegant design, they have often been criticized for not contributing to street life or security.

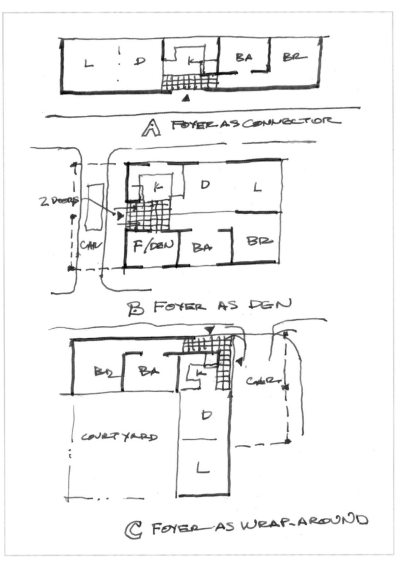

Figure 7.8 Freehand sketches (pen and ink) of different types of foyers and access: foyer as connector between living area and sleeping area (public and private); foyer as den guest room; foyer as wraparound kitchen. Sketches are concept ideas before planning on SketchUp or other computer-assisted drawing (CAD) programs.

Figure 7.9a Basic Foyer, 4 Feet Wide by 12 Feet Long. Bowfront table, oval mirror, etching, and coat pegs. There is also a walk-off carpet, a very important feature for a foyer. Although it is small, this foyer provides all of the necessary entry elements, including an Aalto stool.

Figure 7.9b Medium Foyer, 6 Feet Wide by 12 Feet Long. Wide enough for a bench, a 12-inch coat storage cabinet, and a full-length mirror.

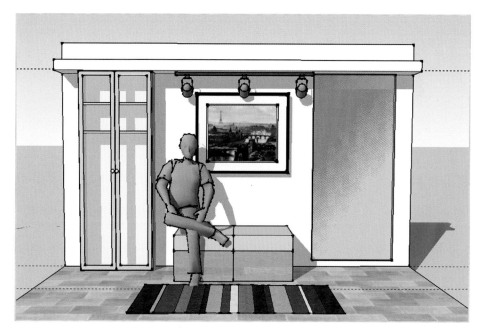

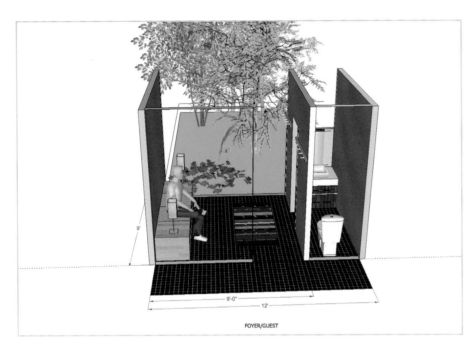

FOYER/GUEST

Figure 7.9c Foyer at 9 Feet by 12 Feet. Furnished as a guest room, with fold-out or slide-out bed. This room can be made private, with its own powder room. It doesn't have a shower though, so guests can't stay too long.

Figure 7.9d This foyer is the same size, 9 feet by 12 feet, but it is furnished for use as a den or home work area. Depending on the location in the house, it can have a yard view.

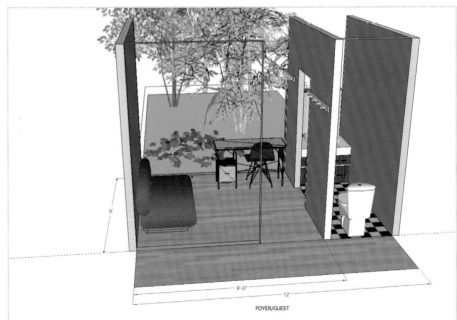

FOYER/GUEST

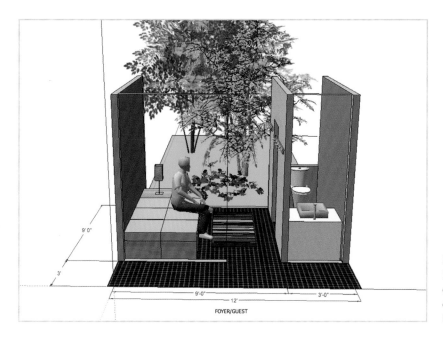

Figure 7.9e An enlarged foyer of 9 feet by 12 feet can include a powder room (lavatory and water closet). It can also accommodate more coats and keep them out of the fray of the corridor. There is enough room for a bench or sofa, and it can double as a reading room.

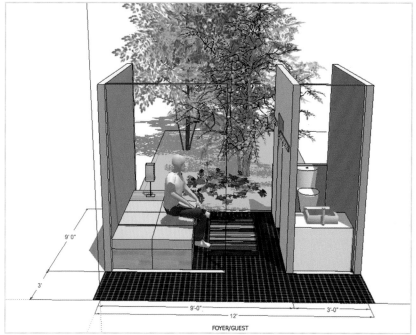

Figure 7.9f Turn on View>Shadows in SketchUp to see how this room looks with sunlight streaming in.

KEY TERMS

Foyer: Area defining the entry to a space. Can be internal or, as in apartment buildings, external.

Digital pen: A stylus attached to your computer that allows you to draw directly onto your digitized images, using programs such as Photoshop.

EXERCISES AND PRACTICE

1. Photograph many different types of foyers with your digital camera. Keep folders, or albums, in iPhoto for easy retrieval.
2. Use the digital pen for making notes on field conditions in existing foyers.
3. In a renovation, you can show your client the advantages and disadvantages of the present foyer and sketch in how you could change it.
4. Explore lobbies and entries to apartment buildings, including corridors for accessing dwelling units.

CHAPTER 8

The Great Room

Objectives

- Learn how to use new SketchUp and Photoshop tools while learning how to plan combined living/dining/food preparation spaces and illuminate them.
- Import 2D images, such as jpegs.
- Use the follow me tool to create walls.
- Learn how to work with the hide and unhide tools.
- Learn how to add task lighting for a home office in Photoshop.

Overview

We will use new SketchUp and Photoshop tools to study how individual room adjacencies can be planned. You can import freehand concept sketches into SketchUp and convert them into models. Do you need to determine which rooms should be located adjacent to each other? Or figure out the sequence for circulation through the home? Or maybe you want to explore different possibilities for living/dining/kitchen spaces. We will use SketchUp to copy and move components and entire rooms from place to place. We will show how the living room can be an open or closed space adjacent to the dining room and how the kitchen and serving area is related to dining and entertainment areas. When this area is wide open, it is called a great room.

Creating the Great Room

The designer usually begins concept drawings as freehand sketches. He or she makes some scribbles or bubble diagrams on a sketchpad or cheap tracing paper, even a napkin, working toward a refined design. These very loose sketches (see Fig. 8.2b) can be imported into SketchUp and then scaled to a measurable rectangle (see Fig. 8.2c). After scaling the plan (Fig. 8.2c), use the sketch walls to indicate where you want to create 3D demising walls in the model. Use the **Follow Me** tool (see Figs. 8.3a and b) to create an exterior wall around the plan. **Hide** the front wall so you can see the plan (see Fig. 8.3c). Then draw a rectangle on the plan the size of the wall footprint and extrude it up to the ceiling height (see Fig. 8.4a). Here you might consider changing the overall general style, or look, of the SketchUp drawing. Go to **Window>Styles** and look at the options available for ground color, background, edge style, and others. This can greatly affect the quality of your image.

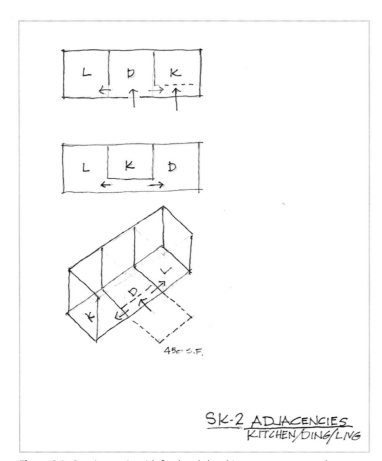

Figure 8.1a Starting again with freehand sketching concepts, we explore different possibilities for adjacencies in living/dining/kitchen space (great room).

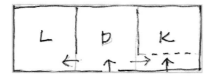

Figure 8.1b Select one. We chose kitchen on right, dining room in center, and living room on left.

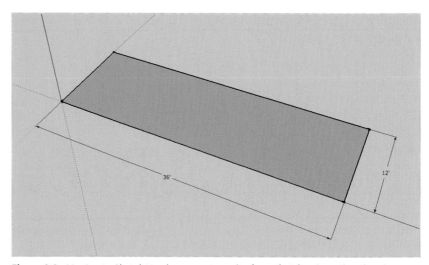

Figure 8.2a Moving to SketchUp, draw a rectangular face of 36 feet by 12 feet for plan.

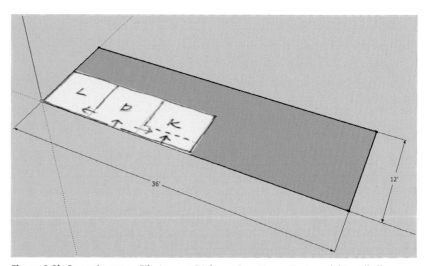

Figure 8.2b Go to the menu File>Import>Dialogue Box>Use as Texture. (This will allow you to stretch the imported image to size.) This works for walls as well as floors.

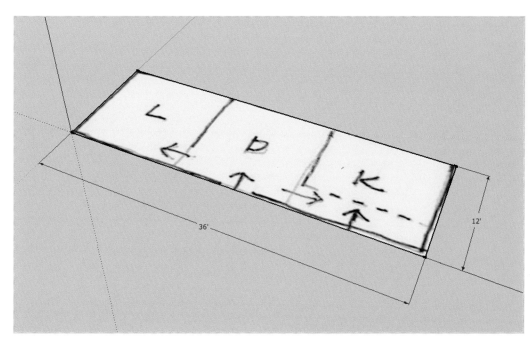

Figure 8.2c Stretch, or Scale, the plan to fill the rectangle of 36 feet by 12 feet.

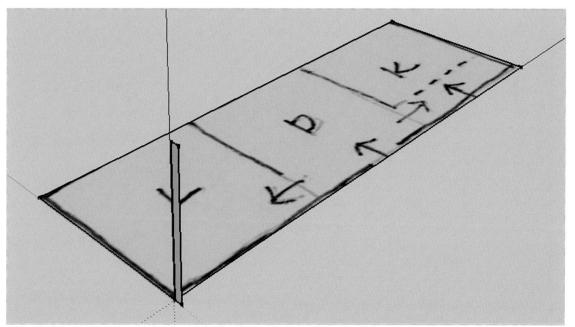

Figure 8.3a Draw a vertical rectangle the size of a wall, for example, 8 feet wide by 9 feet high.

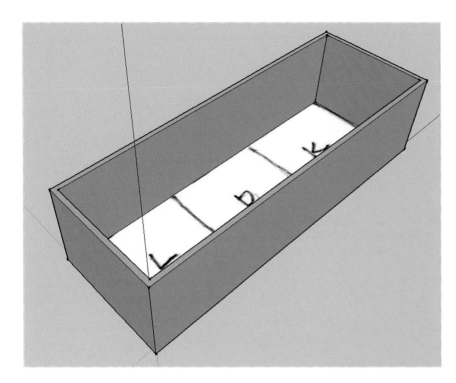

Figure 8.3b Select the Follow Me tool, then select the rectangle and move it around the perimeter of the plan. This is a quick way to draw the perimeter walls.

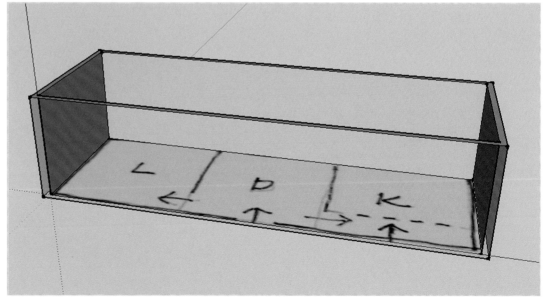

Figure 8.3c Select the front wall. Choose Edit>Hide to make it invisible, so you can work on the interior. When you're done, you can Unhide it, or paint it with a translucent color (low saturation).

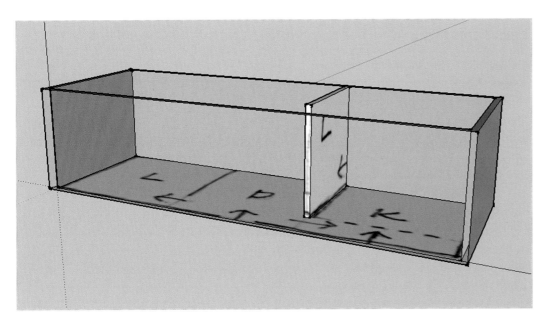

Figure 8.4a If you choose to build a wall between the kitchen and dining areas (a "closed kitchen"), draw a rectangle on the floor where indicated by the sketch. Then extrude (push-pull) it up to 9 feet high.

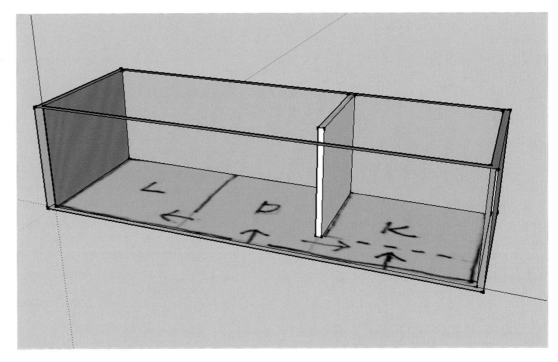

Figure 8.4b The extruded wall will pick up some of the floor markings, so just paint it out. At this point, you might choose to paint out the floor as well and substitute a flooring material.

Now you can begin importing components. You may have some favorites on previous SketchUp files that you can copy and paste into this one. Import or copy kitchen cabinets, appliances, tables, chairs, desks, bookshelves, lamps, carpets, artwork, and even custom-designed furniture you may have already created. Apply different floor finishes for the different spaces. (You will have to draw separate rectangles for each of these floor areas for the finish to apply.) Load some people as well to give scale and a human touch to the renderings. If you don't like the SketchUp people images, you can add realistic figures later in Photoshop.

Hide some of the exterior walls and the ceiling so that you can better visualize the interior. Add some trees and landscape features for an indoor/outdoor environment. The last thing to do is turn on **View>Shadows** to see how your image looks shaded. Shadows take a lot of memory, so they slow down the changes you make. It's best to turn them off when working on the rendering. Remember, you can change the location of the model, the time of day, and calendar date by clicking **Window>Shadow** and opening the dialogue box. Now you can **Save As** another drawing, making use of the work you've done and applying new locations for demising walls. This will allow you to study the different possibilities for space arrangements. When you have one or more views that you like, take a screenshot of it and open it in Photoshop. Repeat this multiple times.

Try several different plans: a closed home office, an open conversation area, and a formal dining room. Save these to Photoshop and use the **Filter>Render>Lighting Effects** tool to create different types of lighting.

When you have started to add furniture to the Living Room, for example, you can **Copy** and **Move** the different pieces of furniture, using the Move tool while holding down option. This creates a copy, and you can move it into place. To turn it in the right direction, use **Rotate**, or click **Edit>Solid Group>Flip Along>Group's Red (or Green) Axis**.

The Living Area

Here are some tips to take into consideration for planning convivial living spaces:

1. Determine the type of living space. Will it be used primarily for entertaining or family gatherings? Or as a quiet space for reading or listening to music? Or as an entertainment center focused around a TV? Will it double as a home office or guest room? This should be determined in advance of conceptual planning by means of a client interview or checklist.

2. Study the type of furniture you will use. Advise your client on the variety of seating available, from sofas to lounge chairs to club chairs. Coffee tables are important too. If you are using it for entertaining, it should be large enough and high enough, at least 18 inches high.

3. Place the seating close enough for conversation. You can place the furniture at a right angle to accommodate conversation that allows for TV viewing at the same time as allowing chatting. Or place chairs and sofas facing each other for conversation only. SketchUp models of these options are shown in this chapter.

4. Side tables are important for placing objects, such as books, lamps, and the ubiquitous remote controls. A sofa and two side tables will measure from 8 feet to 10 feet in length, so be sure you have a wall of at least that length.

5. Is there enough room for a desk in the living room, or is it even desirable?

6. Lighting is very important. Select generalized lighting for the room, but be sure to use individual task lights for reading and desktops. Dimmers are very useful and desirable for all lighting. We will show how you can use PhotoShop Lighting Effects to create the ambience for the room.

Figure 8.5a Populate the great room with furniture, bookshelves, a media wall, lounge seating, and a dining room table and chairs. Copy and Paste the adjoining kitchen from the previous chapter. Also, begin to define the exterior walls. Facing the front is the assumed view area, so it is relatively open and oriented to the south.

Figure 8.5b The left (west) wall is solid to accept the shelving. The north wall is about 30 inches high, as a back for chairs and couch. Shadows come from the southwest, a late afternoon sun. These can be adjusted. Here we learn about Style selection. Go to Window›Styles and look at the options offered for foreground, background, and a wire frame. We selected the Simple Style to show an earthy green and a simulated blue sky that gets lighter at the horizon. You can also go to the Edit tab or the Mix tab and change some of settings. The style changes will show instantly on your model, so you can choose your favorite.

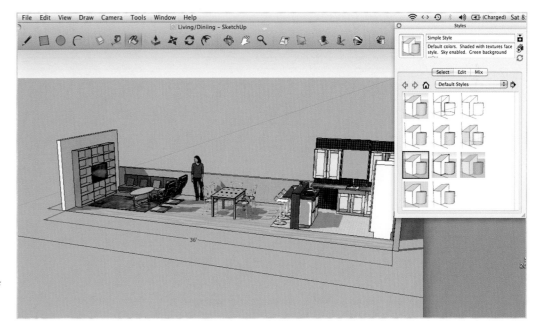

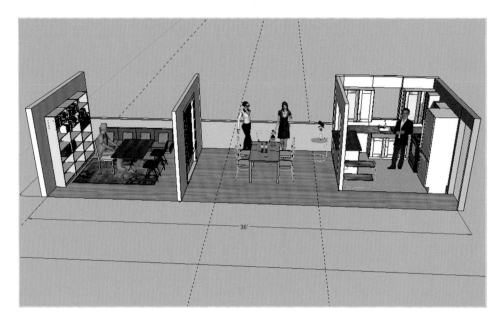

Figure 8.6a A separate study/dining/kitchen or home office. Three separate activities can be going on at the same time. The kitchen has a pass-through opening.

Figure 8.6b Bird's-eye view of the dining/study and part of the kitchen.

Figure 8.6c Dining room and home office as separate rooms. Separated by Prairie-style French doors.

Figure 8.6d Formal dining room. Add a banquette, hanging pendant lights, a formal glass table and chairs, and a landscape.

Figure 8.6e The home office can double as a den or guest room.

Figure 8.6f Home office at night with lighting. Add a desk lamp, some books, and a studious person. Take a screenshot of this view and open it in Photoshop. Then, as previously described in Figure 6.11e, open Filters>Rendering>Lighting Effects and adjust the type of lighting, focus, and, importantly, ambience. This balances the light between the highlighted fixture and the rest of the room. See the dramatic difference this effect makes on rendering.

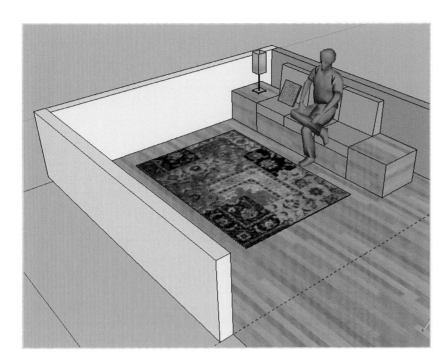

Figure 8.7a A living room can also serve as a conversation area. The seating should be arranged so that people face each other (Figure 8.7d). The bench shown is custom designed and is kept in a separate file.

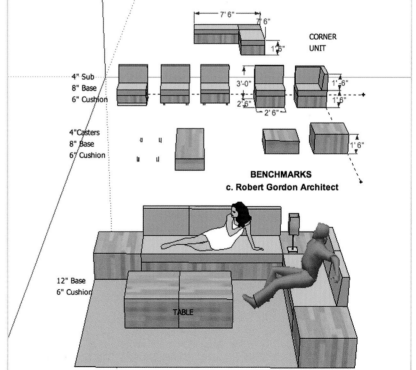

Figure 8.7b Benches are a very convenient way of arranging seating for different size spaces. They don't take up as much room as a conventional sofa or easy chairs, and they can also double as guest sleeping. Here we show the different ways of copying groups or other elements. When they are in two separate files, you can simply Select>Copy and then open the other file and Paste. If the objects are in the same file, it is usually more convenient to Select, use the Move tool, and hold down Option on a Mac or Ctrl on Windows.

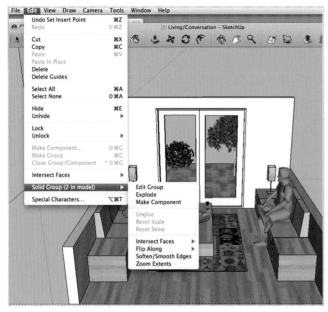

Figure 8.7c Because the focus of the view is other people, there should be seating facing the first bench. This can be achieved easily with the Copy and Flip tools. First, Copy the bench and move it to the opposite side of the room. Select the copied bench, then Edit>Solid Group>Flip Along>Group's Red Axis.

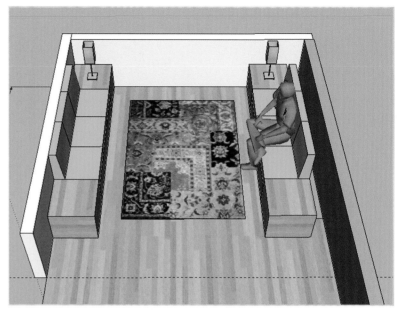

Figure 8.7d The result will be a flipped seating area where people face each other for conversation. These benches are inspired by Frank Lloyd Wright's Usonian houses, where the furniture was designed as part of the house.

Figure 8.7e Now you can add the components to make the room comfortable. Components should include convenience tables (food and drink are always welcome), a landscaped view or yard, and lighting. Use View>Shadows to show late afternoon sunlight. The windows on either side are not yet decided, so space is left for them above the sill level.

See the great room in the Pappageorge Haymes private residence in the Art Gallery in **Chapter 12**. This example also shows the development of digital renderings of this space.

Key Commands Covered in this Chapter

In SketchUp
1. File>Import
2. Follow Me
3. Edit>Solid Group>Flip Along>
4. Window>Styles
5. Simple Style
6. The SketchUp **Copy**, **Paste**, and **Move** tools that we have previously learned allow us to easily compare different alternative schemes.

In Photoshop
1. Filter>Render>Lighting Effect

KEY TERMS

Demising walls: Walls that define rooms or individual spaces.

Task lighting: Lighting focused on individual work areas, such as desks or counters.

Adjacencies: An analysis of which spaces should ideally adjoin each other, allowing the designer to best choose the locations for each space.

EXERCISES AND PRACTICE

1. Sketch several different arrangements for the kitchen, dining, and living areas. Render them with markers.
2. Import the best one into SketchUp and extrude it to full ceiling height.
3. Design at least one piece of custom furniture, such as a chair, table, or sofa. Make a SketchUp file of this item.
4. Photograph a variety of interior spaces. Open at least one in Photoshop and add Lighting Effects to it.

The Kitchen

Objectives

- Learn how SketchUp can be a very useful tool in designing kitchens.
- Review the principles of kitchen design and accessibility based on the National Kitchen and Bath Association.

Overview

A limited number of kitchen plans have been accepted as standard in the industry. These include compact, L-shaped, linear galley style, or island type. What they all have in common is that there should be adequate space to prepare food, cook it, wash dishes, and dispose of trash. Cooking can be surface style sautés or oven roasting. The National Kitchen and Bath Association (NKBA) provides booklets to designers to guide them through the intricacies and meet the standards of the Americans with Disabilities Act.[1]

Designing Kitchens Using SketchUp Components

It has been said that the kitchen is the heart of the home, the hearth. Yet it is a very small space, with many technical requirements, such as ovens, cooktops, refrigeration, dishwashing, trash removal, lighting, and ventilation. The work surfaces must accommodate hot pots and pans, as well as places to cut, mix ingredients, and prepare food. The space also must be adjacent to the dining area for serving and dish removal.

SketchUp provides a wealth of components for kitchens, ranging from Ikea brand to high-end cabinets and appliances. There's even one component with bacon and eggs and the morning paper on the counter-top. You can download specific appliances through the components menu of SketchUp, and some companies supply 3D models from their websites, which can be downloaded through the Google Warehouse. (**Tip**: Create a SketchUp drawing that includes many of these different components that you can copy and paste into any new kitchen you are designing. It takes less time than searching for the components from scratch.)

---

1. The National Kitchen and Bath Association, "Kitchen and Bathroom Planning Guidelines with Access Standards," latest edition.

Kitchen Types

The *compact kitchen* is a prefabricated kitchen of 5 feet to 6 feet in length, containing a cooktop, oven, sink, and under-counter refrigerator, which can be used in places that are not large enough to accommodate full-sized refrigerators. A 6-by-6-foot room can be adequate for a kitchen. It can also be very convenient for starter houses or emergency facilities. SketchUp includes this unit in its components menu.

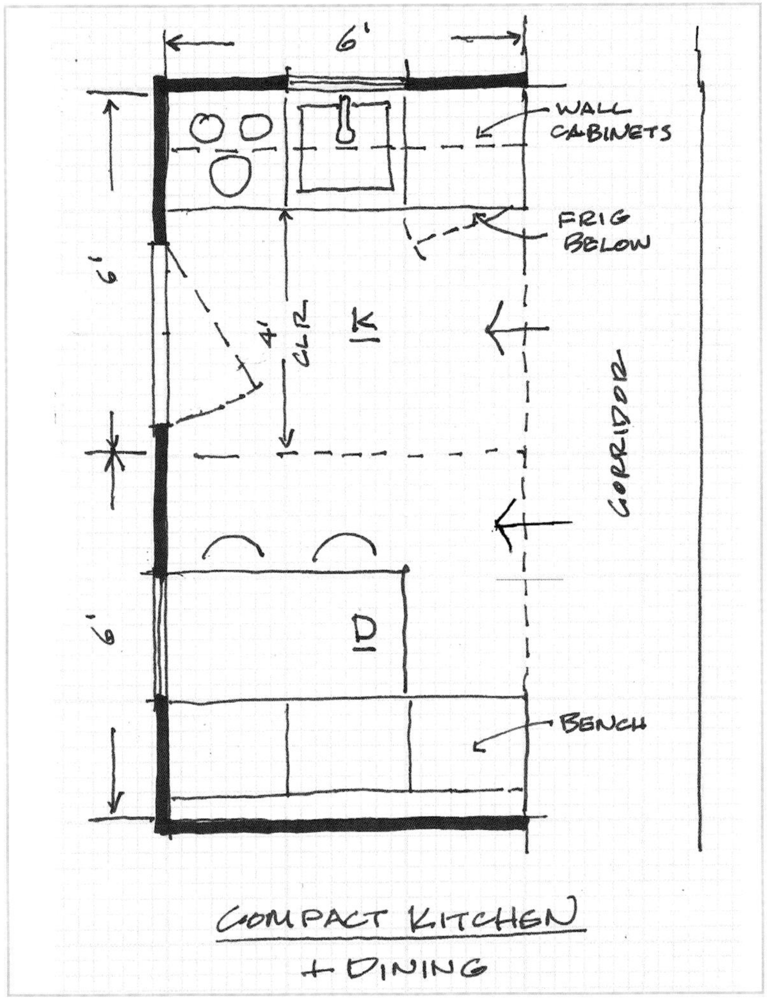

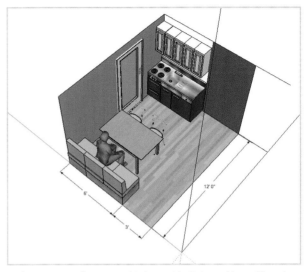

Figure 9.2a Bird's-eye view of compact kitchen with dining table and bench seating.

Figure 9.2b View of compact kitchen with interior finishing. Shows pendant light, plates, flower vase, painting, landscaped yard, and a young couple. All of these are standard Google Warehouse components. A custom-designed bench is used for compact seating (and an extra bed).

Figure 9.1 Compact Kitchen Plan, 6 by 6 feet. Known as the "coin cuisine" in France because it sits in a corner of the room. There are several manufacturers who make the range, sink, and under-counter refrigerator all in one unit. It's ideal for a small space or studio apartment. Plan views show how it can be combined with a compact dining area.

An *island kitchen* is shown in Figures 9.3a–d. This plan includes a bar-height counter for service to the dining room. Several different views show the kitchen at different angles.

The *Ikea kitchen* shown in Figures 9.4 to 9.6 is U-shaped. It shows a pass-through rather than an island for access to the dining room. This provides a more enclosed and private food preparation area. Ikea makes

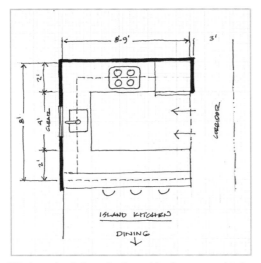

Figure 9.3a Island kitchen plan (9 by 12 feet) provides for an open kitchen and bar between food preparation and living-dining space.

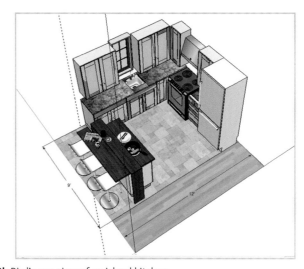

Figure 9.3b Bird's-eye view of an island kitchen.

Figure 9.3c Top view close up of an island kitchen. Shows bar, bacon and eggs, and stone floor with adjoining wood floor. All Google Warehouse components.

Figure 9.3d Eye-level view of kitchen with people (also from Google Warehouse). Shows window over the sink.

a large variety of cabinet doors for any kitchen style. They also make 39-inch-high wall cabinets that maximize the storage for 8-foot ceiling heights. Ikea has its own program, similar to SketchUp, that uses its own components. It also creates a cost estimate sheet that is coordinated with the plan. All you have to do is order the prepared plan and pay for it. The cabinets are delivered flat-packed and can be assembled at the site. Ikea cabinets are well represented in SketchUp components.

(See Pappageorge Haymes private residence kitchen design and SketchUp rendering technique in **Chapter 12**, Single-Family Homes.)

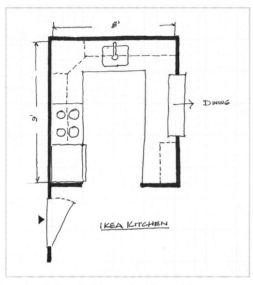

Figure 9.4 Ikea kitchen plan designed with standard Ikea cabinets.

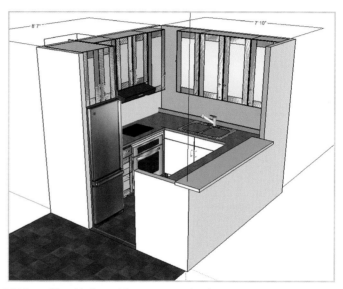

Figure 9.5 View of Ikea kitchen with an open peninsula counter.

Figure 9.6 Photo of finished Ikea kitchen with white Ikea cabinets and lighting, as well as hanging utensil bars and granite countertops.

Galley kitchen: An inline galley kitchen that is usually arranged along a wall and includes all mechanical and electrical connections.

Kitchen island: An open kitchen with a base cabinet and countertop. The island can be either 36-inch or 42-inch counter height. The bar height will hide any preparation items from view in the dining room.

Pass-through: When a more private food preparation is desired, a wall can be opened to allow serving food to the dining room and removing dirty dishes.

1. Using the NKBA handbook, design several different kitchen types using the specified clearances. Download SketchUp files for this purpose.
2. By using SketchUp techniques, show the effect of placing a window in the kitchen.

CHAPTER 10

The Bathroom

Objectives

- Use SketchUp to examine different types and sizes of bathrooms.
- Understand how different types and sizes of bathrooms affect the planning for the rest of the unit.

How We Use Bathrooms, Toilet Rooms, and Powder Rooms

It may seem obvious to most of us that an indoor "bath" room is crucial to the modern concept of comfort in a home. The term *bathroom* is a euphemism, because we know that much more than bathing goes on in this room, but indoor plumbing is a relatively recent development in the history of human habitation and comfort. The Romans bathed outdoors and enjoyed it in the warm climate. Outhouses were the prevalent form of waste disposal throughout Europe and the United States until the 20th century. Apartment dwellers in New York tenements had to run down to the backyard and wait their turn.

Early versions of the indoor toilet room were called "crappers" in honor of the inventor, Thomas Crapper, who popularized the indoor water closet. In the United States following the Second World War, compact indoor bathrooms were a requisite for all new homes being built, but they were very small, usually about 35 square feet, and the water closet, or toilet, was jammed right up next to the lavatory and bathtub.

The Europeans use separate rooms for water closets and lavatory/tubs. This is more sanitary and also cuts down on traffic jams for the toilet/bathroom.

We will explore these different types of bathrooms, including the addition of a washer/dryer, and see how they look with Google SketchUp. We will first create a 12-by-12-foot floor module, and then push-pull or extrude it to 6 inches thick, using SketchUp. Then, we will select a floor finish and make a Group out of this floor (as described in **Chapter 4**), so we can move walls around on it.

Now design a 5-by-9-foot (45 square feet) basic bathroom, including toilet, lavatory, and tub. Separate the toilet from the washing/bathing area with a wall, and create separate doors for each space. We haven't added area to the room, but we have greatly increased the privacy for family members. This is easily shown in 3D with SketchUp.

Let's expand the bathroom into a suite to include a walk-in shower and a washer/dryer combination unit. The area of this space is 12 feet by 9 feet, or 108 square feet. This adds only 63 square feet to the bathroom area, but it also adds great utility. It is especially useful for multiple users of a residential unit. (**Tip**: The components used in the basic bathroom can be saved, or the file can be Saved As for the larger suite. This precludes the need to search for components each time.)

See Pappageorge Haymes private residence in **Chapter 12** for master bathroom design and SketchUp rendering technique.

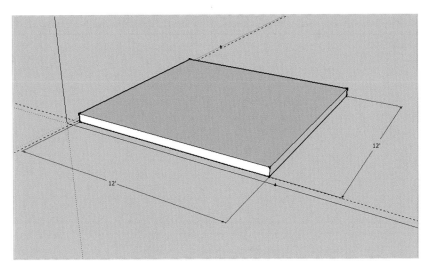

Figure 10.1 The module shown here is a 12-by-12-foot concrete slab, 6 inches thick. It forms the basis for this room and others shown in Part III. First, draw the square with the Rectangle tool, then Push-Pull it up 6 inches. At this point, turn it into a Group, so it's easier to move the wall around on it.

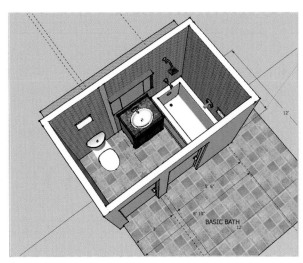

Figure 10.2 Basic Bathroom, 5 feet by 9 feet. It provides basic comforts in a minimum of space. Note that the tub faucet is on the side wall. That makes it easier to turn the water on and off while soaking. Also, there is a niche in the wall to accommodate soaps and shampoos.

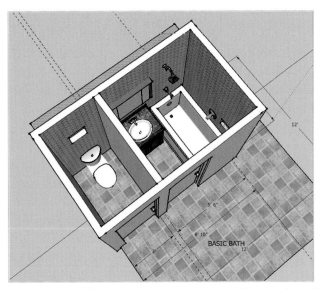

Figure 10.3 Separated Bath. Now, with the same size, 5 feet by 9 feet, place a dividing wall between the water closet and the bathing/washing room. This is very important for privacy, and it doesn't take up additional space.

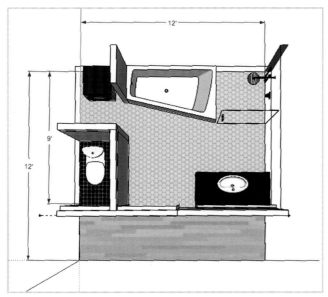

Figure 10.4a Bathroom suite, plan. At 9 feet by 12 feet, it is large enough to accommodate a soaking tub, a shower, a 60-inch vanity, and a mirror. It also affords a separate, private stall for the toilet and a utility closet in the bathroom for a washer/dryer. A European-style unit, such as Miele, with a compact 24-by-24-inch profile fits neatly into closets and under kitchen counters. They run one complete cycle for washing and drying.

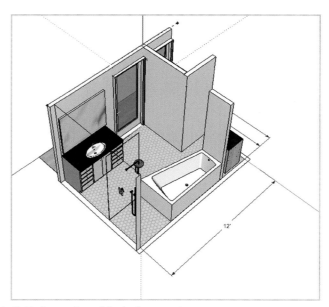

Figure 10.4b Bird's-eye view of the bathroom suite.

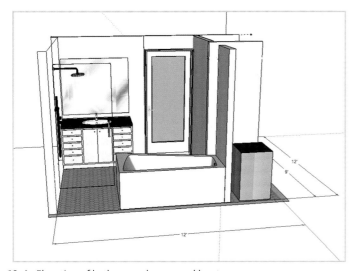

Figure 10.4c Elevation of bathroom, shower, and lavatory.

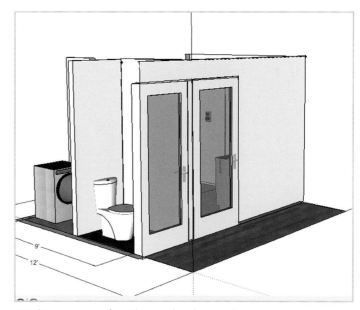

Figure 10.4d Cutaway view from the corridor, showing the separate water closet and the washer/dryer in closet.

KEY TERMS

Powder room: Normally a small room with a water closet and lavatory only, usually located near or in the foyer. The nose-powdering function is no longer prevalent, but the term prevails. Today, we would probably just call it a half-bath.

Group: As described in **Chapter 4**, Groups are created in SketchUp to act as one unit and avoid interference with walls and other elements.

EXERCISES AND PRACTICE

1. Sketch or photograph different types of bathrooms you might like to use in your designs.
2. Keep a file of plumbing fixtures and faucets that are on the market. Sometimes the manufacturers provide SketchUp models that you can download.
3. Research the types and sizes of soaking tubs available, including claw-foot tubs.
4. Try a plan with the tub away from the wall.
5. Try a picture window with an open and private view, like the ocean or mountains.
6. Some bathrooms are now being shown as open to the bedrooms. How would you achieve the necessary balance between privacy and openness?
7. Try a lavatory completely removed from the water closet and tub areas, out in the bedroom.

CHAPTER 11

The Bedroom and Study

Objectives

- Learn how to analyze clients' programmatic and design needs for bedroom suites.
- Integrate freehand concept sketches through SketchUp models and Photoshop finishing for the bedroom and study.
- Learn a variety of different configurations for adjacencies of sleeping, study, clothes, and laundry spaces.
- Use the Lighting Effects filter of Photoshop to see how lighting can affect the mood of a room.

Overview

We will use digital tools to assist in studying how individual bedroom suite adjacencies can be planned. We will explore different possibilities for sleeping, study, closet, bathroom, and laundry spaces. In this chapter, we will review different options for these personal, intimate spaces, making use of the lighting and shadow tools. Final selection is determined by the client's needs and budget.

The standard, or basic, bedroom minimally consists of one or two beds, two night tables, two reading lamps, and a clothes closet (built-in or an armoire). The standard 12-by-12-foot module we have been using is adequate for these needs. It is economical, efficient, and widely used by developers. Because of the circulation space between the bed and the closet, this size makes good use of space. However, if two people are sharing the bedroom, the organization of clothes storage can become an issue. Open closet doors can annoy people, with clothes sometimes left out on the edge of the bed, or other personal idiosyncrasies. If affordable, it would be better to use a walk-in closet or dressing room adjoining the bedroom.

Study/Closet Room

The bedroom becomes more spacious if it doesn't include a closet. You can add a lounge chair for reading or a low credenza. By moving the closet function out of the bedroom and creating a separate room, you can also incorporate a study in the second room. You can create two separate small study/closet rooms.

Study or Home Office

You can create one larger study with less area for clothes storage. This works better for a single person, providing a generous private office and a spacious, uncluttered bedroom. The study can accommodate bookshelves, a desk, a desk lamp, as well as a clothes closet and supply cabinet. Use the **Photoshop Filter>Render>Lighting Effects** tool to show a client how a room would look with a task lamp on a desk. You should also explore generalized lighting in the ceiling, such as wall sconces,

and/or inside the armoires. Many interesting LED lights are available that are automatically switched on as closet doors or drawers are opened.

Ideally, the bedroom suite is adjacent to a bathroom or master bathroom suite. This should also include a laundry area, because it adjoins clothes storage areas. By locating the bathroom adjoining the bedroom/study area in the direction of the main living areas, it serves as a separation between public and private spaces in a home. We will show how this works for various house plans in **Chapter 13**.

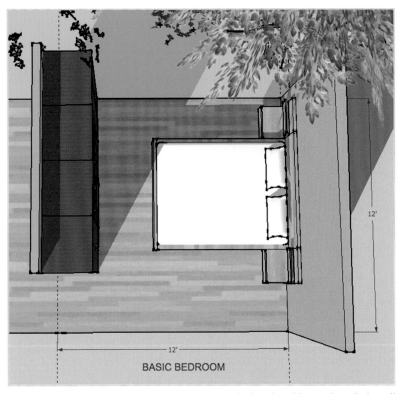

Figure 11.1a Basic bedroom, bird's-eye plan, showing bed, night tables, and wardrobes all in the same room. The space is tight but economical.

Figure 11.1b Basic bedroom, view of wardrobe from Google SketchUp Components Library.

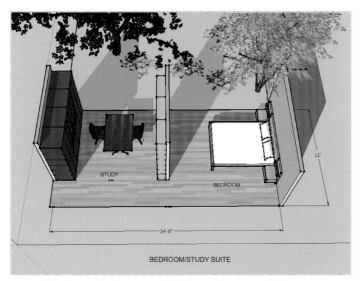

Figure 11.2 Study adjoining bedroom, with shelves and two wardrobes.

Figure 11.3 Bedroom with two adjoining dressing rooms for two people.

Figure 11.4 Study at Night. Add a desk lamp, some books, and a studious person. Take a screenshot of this view and open it in Photoshop. Then, as previously described in Figures 6.11e and 6.11f, open Filter>Render>Lighting Effects. Then adjust the type of lighting, focus, and, importantly ambience. This will balance the light between the highlighted fixture and the rest of the room.

Armoire: A free-standing cabinet serving as a clothes closet and shelving.

LED lights: Light-Emitting Diode lighting. Very energy-efficient and cool lighting. Can be formed into strips of small bulbs, which is ideal for under cabinets, inside closets, and decorative uses.

1. Sketch a variety of options for adjacency of bedroom, bathroom, study, closet, and laundry functions. Be free. For example, try lavatories outside of the water closet and bathrooms, such as are used in some hotels.

2. Show how a bedroom with two beds is different from one with a full or queen-sized bed shared by two people. Should you place night tables on either side of the beds with a storage table or bookshelf between them?

3. Show how a bedroom can share functions with a study by incorporating a desk and chair into the room.

CHAPTER 12

Single-Family Homes

Objectives

- Learn how to use the modular room arrangements and adjacency combinations studied in previous chapters to create a variety of different single-family house types.
- Learn how to use an integration of freehand sketching, SketchUp, and Photoshop to illustrate a variety of different single-family house types.
- Learn how different lot sizes and shapes affect the interior design.

Overview

This chapter explores using Freehand Sketching, SketchUp, and Photoshop to arrange and combine spaces with proper adjacencies. These will form a comprehensive series of housing types for a variety of single-family home sites (high-density urban sites will be explored in the next chapter on townhouses and apartments). This chapter explores different housing types and site relationships as follows:

- Site/landscape plans
- A simple house: The core

- Bungalow
- L-house
- H-house
- H-house, two-story
- Hillside house

Site Planning

From the site diagrams in Figures 12.1a and 12.1b, we will examine appropriate lots for designing four different types of single-family homes. The site diagram in Figure 12.1a shows with a bubble diagram the considerations that affect the layouts of homes on narrow 25-foot lots, as well as the opportunities for 50-foot corner lots. The site plan in Figure 12.1b shows how the four different house types to be described fit on the sites. These site plans will help you understand the basic context in which the different homes are designed, including the approaches. You will see how the pedestrian and vehicular access to homes and parking affect the floor plans.

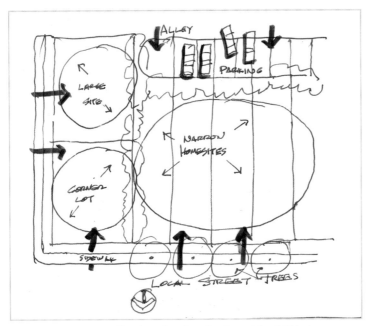

Figure 12.1a General layout of land use for a low-density residential block.

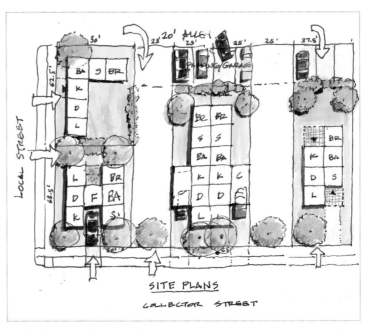

Figure 12.1b Site Plans. The potential for a variety of one-story housing types for a typical block. Plans for a simple house and a bungalow. Site plan of one-story H- and L-houses for larger 50-foot corner lots and I-house for narrow 25-foot lots. Using a zero lot line on one side, a side yard and driveway can be used for a carport or additional yard space. It's also more economical construction to back up the two units as a duplex.

Preliminary Considerations

Before beginning to consider any design project, there is much work to do. Every project needs the following six essential elements:

1. *Client.* We will consider a variety of possible client types: the nuclear family, the blended family (parents and children from previous spouses), single people living together, live/work situations, and single room occupancies.
2. *Program.* The programs for the different designs in this book will vary. Individual room sizes will be programmed, as well as the overall home. In the interest of sustainability, the spaces will be somewhat tight.
3. *Budget.* Mostly, we will try to be frugal. This is often what clients desire. They can always spend more money if they wish to do so.
4. *Site.* This chapter discusses some of the considerations to site selection: urban high density, medium density, and low suburban or rural. To a large extent, this is determined by the client's wishes and budget. Sometimes the designer is asked to participate in a site search, which allows more input.
5. *Contract.* This sets the terms of the relationship between client and architect/designer.
6. *Retainer.* A cash deposit for the work to be done is essential for a serious business relationship.

Single-Family Houses

It was formerly the aspiration for most Americans to own a single, detached home; it was the American dream. The ideal home was typically located on a separate lot, with setbacks at front, rear, and side yards and ample landscaping, with a good school nearby. No dangers lurked. Today, that dream has begun to seem like a quaint, nostalgic trip to the 1950s. Since then, many factors have begun to impact the dream. First, many Americans can no longer afford large houses in the suburbs. It is becoming difficult to find employment in low-density areas without a long commute. Along with the rising cost of fuel for commuting, the rising costs of land and construction, our ability to build single-family homes has eroded. According to McIlwain and Floca, writing in 2006 for the Urban Land Institute, "the median size of the new American home is going to begin to decrease."[1]

Second, the definition of the American family has evolved. No longer does it consist of the proverbial mom, pop, and two children; a typical household, containing a working father, stay-at-home mother, and two children of the same parents now makes up only slightly more than 10% of total households.[2] The typical family has instead become a blended family. As home designers, we are now faced with more families having two different sets of parents and living only part-time in one household or the other. There are father- and mother-in-law spaces, as well as space for adult children returning home after college without jobs. There are households made up of single adults and single cohabiting adults. And there are individuals who prefer to live alone in single-room occupancies. This changing definition of the household requires a rethinking of privacy standards, as well as programmatic needs for a smaller, more efficient footprint. The houses previewed in this chapter take into account these evolving standards.

Figure 12.1c Single-family residences in Chicago, with wide setbacks and trees.

Figure 12.1d Bungalow with front entry in Chicago.

1. John McIlwaine and Melissa Floca, *Multifamily Trends* (Washington DC: Urban Land Institute, 2006).

2. Gwendolyn Wright, *Building the Dream* (Cambridge, MA: MIT Press, 1981), p. xviii.

A Simple House

A simple, narrow house can be a very affordable starter house. It can also be used as an additional unit for a larger lot to accommodate an adult family member or a rental unit. The simple house described here is a narrow house. The rooms and spaces in this house are exactly the same size as the ones in the larger houses. The larger houses have more rooms, such as an extra bedroom, study, and foyer, but they are all within the 12′ x 12′ module. The basic house can be as small as 750 to 900 square feet. With additions, it can be expanded to 1050 square feet, still a "simple house." The advantages of a narrow house can be best seen on a narrow lot, or the leftover space from a larger lot. It also would work well on a shallow lot, which is not very deep from front to back. It is narrow enough to be built in a factory and hauled to the site if that proves economical. Every room or space can have a fully open view to a yard or garden. There is enough room for a carport or pedestrian entry on the side, instead of the front or rear of the house. The simple house in this chapter is shown at times with hidden exterior walls and roof, so that the viewer can better envision the interior. Experiment freely with the landscape components and **Shadow** tool from SketchUp. Show where you would suggest parking an automobile; it could be either on the site or in front of the house.

Figure 12.2a A Simple House. A narrow house for a narrow site. Shown in line drawing.

Figure 12.2b This plan allow driveways, side entries (which are more efficient in the plan), and a generous perimeter of yard space. Fits on a lot that is 25 feet by 125 feet. It can be 700 to 1,050 square feet of floor area. (Some exterior walls have been hidden to show interior furnishings.) Shown in color rendering with markers and colored pencils.

Figure 12.2c Site Plan of Simple House. Shows relation to the street, the alley (parking), and the additional landscaped yard space. Side entry through foyer.

Figures 12.2d and 12.2e Narrow Creole Houses in New Orleans. Here are two examples of simple, narrow homes in New Orleans, called Creole Houses, which, although narrow, provide a practical and economical dwelling for many people. These good starter houses have a strong and colorful presence on the streetscape.

The One-Story Bungalow

The bungalow is one of the most ubiquitous houses you can find in most cities and suburbs. It follows the same programmatic rules as the simple house, but it is twice as wide (about 25 feet) with the same area, usually from 900 to 1,200 square feet.

Figures 12.3a and 12.3b Bungalow. A 1,200-square-foot, two- or three-bedroom house for a 25-foot lot. Drawn over a SketchUp model in Black and White and rendered in color with markers and colored pencils. Normally, one enters a bungalow from the front, although on a wide lot a side entry is desirable. A site with an alley in back is ideal for on-site parking or a garage.

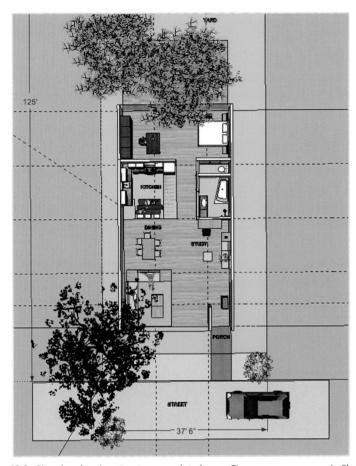

Figure 12.3c Site plan showing street approach to house. Figures 12.3c–12.3e are in SketchUp.

Figure 12.3d Floor Plan

Figure 12.3e Bird's-eye view of bungalow rendered in SketchUp, with hidden roof. Compare with hand drawing in Fig. 12.3b.

The front of the bungalow is usually the living/dining space with exposure to the street, while the rear is reserved for private spaces like bedrooms or studies. If there is a need for two bedrooms, they will each be about 12 feet wide. Or you could combine them into one large master bedroom/study, as shown in Figure 12.3d.

Define the lot size with a new rectangle. Color this distinctly green using the **Materials** tool. (**Tip**: It's best to stick with the **Crayon Box** color tool to minimize the number of colors you use so you can find them easily later.)

This house is greatly affected by the landscape, so get out the **Components** tool and search for different types of trees, shrubs, and flowers. Select cars and people as well. There are many from which to choose. Save the front façade from SketchUp as a jpeg and open it in Photoshop. From here, you can use your digital pen to sketch roof and attic possibilities.

Hide the exterior walls and roof to work on the interior spaces. You can zoom in close to examine different rooms, furniture arrangements, and finishes. Views from the rear garden into the bedroom/study can be especially useful. Make screenshots to record the different views. Or add specific views through the **View>Animation>Scenes** tool in SketchUp. After you're done, simply **Unhide All**. Turn the **Shadow** tool on and off to see the effects of shadows at different times of the day. (**Tip:** If you're unsure which version you prefer, or want to show options to your client, save your SketchUp file with a new name. This will give your client a fine array of choices for interior planning, furniture selection and arrangement, finishing and colors, as well as the shadows at different times of the day. Don't create too many versions as to be overwhelming, just enough to show the possibilities that you as a designer would offer.)

A Courtyard House

A courtyard house can be of many different forms; a courtyard in the center of the house like an atrium is common. In our case study, we are looking at an L-shaped house that turns its back on the street and alley and opens onto an interior garden. Go to Figure 12.1b and look in the upper left-hand corner of the site plan. You will find a site 62.5 feet wide by 50 feet deep. If the adjoining alley is a route for garbage pickup and other services, as well as parking, as it is in many places, it may not be a desirable side to face. So the house is shaped to be oriented toward the interior garden.

Try starting with a freehand line drawing for your initial concept. You can then render it in markers and colored pencils to show your client. Once it is generally approved, you can be more precise with a SketchUp model. Draw a plan with the **Camera>Standard Views>Top**. Use the **Dimension** tool to show dimensions of the rooms and overall house. Choose furniture to import from the **Components** library. Select an array of landscape objects: trees, shrubs, flowers, and outdoor furniture. Use them to enhance the interior garden you have created. Select a car to place in the driveway and figures to enliven the scene. Concentrate on views of people using the garden, because this is the focus of your design. Work with walls and roof off while you are adding furniture and finishes. When that's done, you can place the walls back in as we have done in previous examples. (**Tip:** Remember you can always Hide and Unhide parts of the model for better viewing. Take many screenshots so you can show how the house looks on the interior as you are going through the process and changing things.)

Figures 12.4a and 12.4b Courtyard House. A 1,050-square-foot house, line drawing, then rendered with markers and colored pencils. Ideal for site oriented toward the interior. Compact yet split plan is spacious.

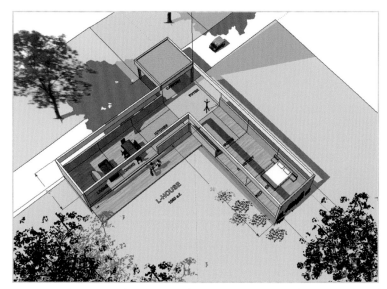

Figure 12.4c Bird's-eye view showing room layouts, with an optional study or enlarged bedroom. Carport on the side, foyer at the corner. Figures 12.4c–12.4k are in SketchUp.

Figure 12.4d Oblique view above the yard.

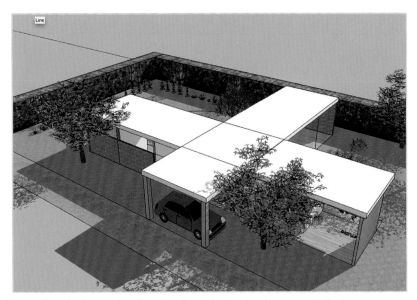

Figure 12.4e Bird's-eye view from the street showing landscaping and shadows.

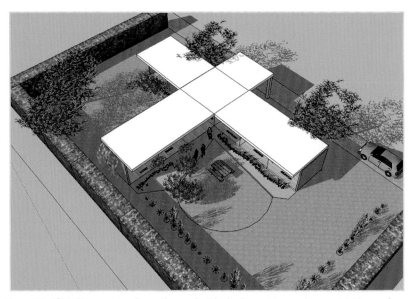

Figure 12.4f Bird's-eye view above the yard with shadows. House shown with the roof. The flower group component was brought in.

Figure 12.4g Yard view showing sloping site.

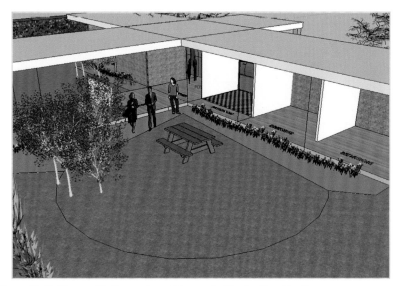

Figure 12.4h Closeup bird's-eye view of the yard with planting. The flower group component was brought in.

Figure 12.4i Eye-level view of entry carport.

Figure 12.4j Eye-level view of living/dining terrace from the yard.

Figure 12.4k Eye-level view of the courtyard.

The H House: A Corner House with Split Plan

Again, working with a lot size of 50 feet wide by 62.5 feet deep, we can alter the circulation and orientation of the house while using the same room sizes and adjacencies. Go to Figure 12.1b and look at the lower left-hand corner. This is a corner lot, so it has exposure on two sides. Assuming a carport or driveway on the 50-foot side, use the foyer to divide the house into two different zones: the great room and the bedroom suite. This splits the home into a formal, public zone for adults entertaining and a quiet zone for family members who may be studying or sleeping. It also creates an interesting variety of yard spaces and indoor/outdoor patios.

As with the previous courtyard house, use the landscape components to emphasize the garden space. Use different floor finishes to delineate indoor floors from outdoor tile or concrete floors. Also show how you can provide a roof over the rear patio and create an outdoor space that's protected from the rain and direct sunlight—an adventure in indoor/outdoor living.

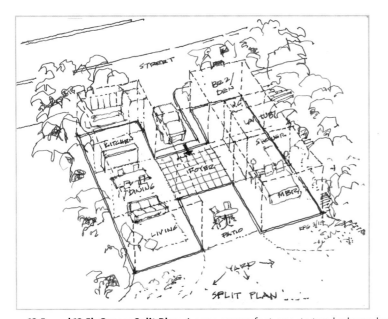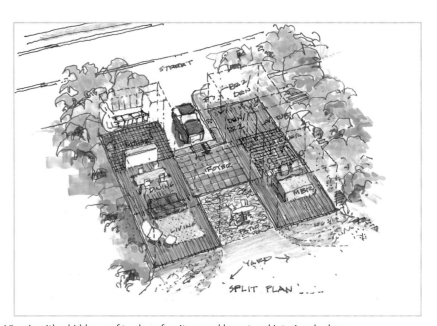

Figures 12.5a and 12.5b Corner Split Plan. A 1,050-square-foot, one- to two-bedroom house. View is with a hidden roof to show furniture and layout and interior shadows.

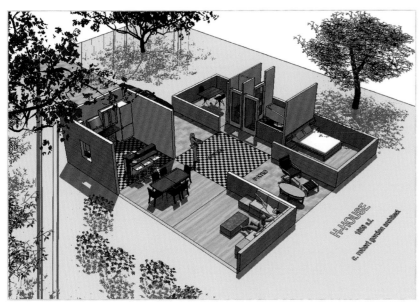

Figure 12.5c Bird's-eye view in SketchUp with roof hidden to show plan.

Figures 12.6a and 12.6b A 1,050-square-foot second floor for a total of 2,100 square feet. House has four bedrooms and three baths.

The Two-Story Split-Plan House

A prime corner lot offers the opportunity for a larger house. When a family grows, a second story can be added, as long as provision has been made for an adequate foundation. First draw freehand sketches. Use SketchUp tools and the digital pen to finish the concepts.

Create a Save As file (for a two-story model) in SketchUp. Draw the second floor over the first floor plan and leave it white. On this model, sketch the layout of the rooms, as you want them. It's best to stack the bathrooms for economy of plumbing. Designate an area in the Foyer for the stairway. (**Tip**: Hold down the Shift key while drawing a line with the digital pen, and it will keep the line straight on the x- or y-axis.)

Now do a Copy and Paste of the first floor to reuse some of the walls you have modeled. You can easily delete them if you don't want them on the second floor. Hide some of the exterior walls so you can see the interior atrium/stairway in section. Save this image as a jpeg and open it in Photoshop. Create a new layer called stairway. Use the digital pen to sketch how you would generally like the stairway to circulate up through the atrium. You can turn off the other layers and look at just the stairway sketch if you wish. You can even enhance it here.

Now go back to the Foyer in SketchUp, but view it from the front of the house as a bird's-eye. Turn the opacity of the second floor very low, about 30 percent, so you can see what's under it on the first floor. Take a screenshot of this, open it in Photoshop, and sketch the atrium stairway. Finish the house in SketchUp, creating a Prairie style design with cantilevered terraces and overhanging roofs. When you're done with this, draw some roofs on the spaces to show how the house looks from the exterior

from both streets on the corner as well as a bird's-eye view. Add landscaping and shadows. Show people and cars at the front entry. You may leave the guidelines for texture or remove them as you please.

The two-story split-plan house is ideal for the new type of client, the blended family or even the single individual. It can be used as a large single-family house of 2,100 square feet or made into two 900-square-foot flats (connected by an atrium stairway) by converting one of the second-floor bathrooms into a kitchen. Finally, it can be made into four individual one-bedroom units with a kitchen/bathroom core in the center of each flat.

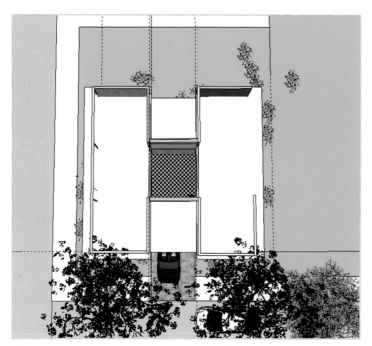

Figure 12.6c Second floor base for plan (first floor similar to previous house).

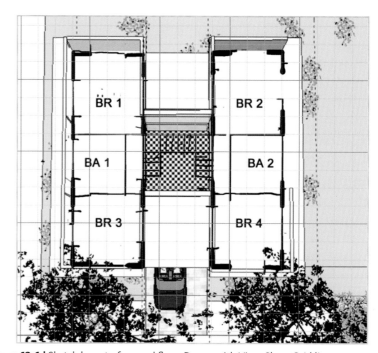

Figure 12.6d Sketch layout of second floor. Drawn with View>Show Grid lines.

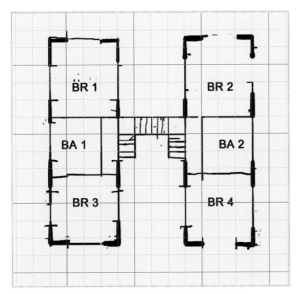

Figure 12.6e Separate plan from SketchUp Image.

Figure 12.6f Side walls are hidden to show center atrium for stairway planning.

Figure 12.6g Freehand sketch of stairway on SketchUp model.

Figure 12.6h Hide SketchUp layer on Photoshop to show freehand sketch alone.

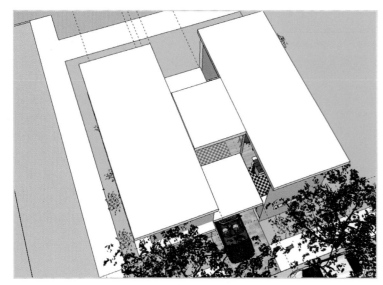

Figure 12.6i Bird's-eye view showing roof plan. Carport and patio roofs are at first floor level, whereas stairway and bedroom roofs are at second floor level.

Figure 12.6j Bird's-eye view of entry court from street showing glass façade.

Figure 12.6k Foyer Top View. This view helps visualize the atrium area where the stairway will be added.

Figure 12.6l Showing glass façade at stairway entry above carport.

Figure 12.6m Sketch stairway over foyer layer, top view.

Figure 12.6n Massing model, front view in SketchUp.

Figure 12.6o Massing model, corner street view.

The "Hillside" or Hilltop View House

Certain sites give us rare opportunities to view distant panoramas at the horizon. Houses near hilltops are one such possibility. There are several ways to use this type of site, depending on how large it is. The house can be slightly curved, adjusting to the panorama. Or you can take elements of the house with which we are already familiar and angle them toward specific views. The foyer can be stretched and/or angled to accommodate this twisting of the spaces. The hillside house in Oakland Hills, viewed in Figures 6.7a–c, shows a version of the curved house from the street below, and Figure 12.7 shows a staggered, angled version.

Tools

- SketchUp concepts
- Digital pen overlays for freehand sketching on SketchUp models
- Landscape components
- Photoshop enhancements

Figure 12.7 Bird's-eye floor plan showing separation of elements for wide views.

KEY TERMS

Bungalow: Single-family home with all of the living space on one level. A basement or attic can be added for storage or a shop. Named after *bangla* or *bangala*, a type of house in the Indian province of Bengal.

X- or Y-axis: X usually refers to the axis from left to right, while Y refers to top to bottom on a drawing. (Actual vertical axis is usually Z.)

Prairie style: A popular style of the early to mid-20th century in the United States, which featured horizontal lines and overhanging roofs and was often associated with Frank Lloyd Wright. Named because of its association with the horizontal lines of the prairies.

Cantilever: An overhang, such as in a roof or terrace, that passes over its supports and has no columns on its perimeter.

Panorama: A very wide view, usually of a landscape.

Sandbox: A set of tools for creating contour models of terrain. This menu can be left on the screen. (See Patrick Rosen's Dunes House in this chapter's Art Gallery.)

EXERCISES AND PRACTICE

1. Draw a narrow house, about 12 feet wide on the interior, for a 25-foot lot. Surround the lot with courtyard walls the height of the building walls. Try stretching out the interior to create small, private gardens.
2. Show how opening up a stairway to the attic of a bungalow can increase its usability. Use skylights and dormers to add light to the attic.
3. Show pitched roofs for the split-plan house by sketching over the model with flat roofs. Draw them freehand or with a digital pen.
4. Photograph a panoramic view that you like. Collage it, either digitally or by hand, to be seen through the windows of a view house.

ART GALLERY

The following single-family homes are featured:

- Private residence by Pappageorge Haymes
- Dunes House by Patrick Rosen
- Lincoln Park addition by Patrick Rosen

Single-Family Private Residence by Pappageorge Haymes Architects

This two-story, masonry brick home is situated in the popular DePaul area of Chicago's Lincoln Park community. It has a 5,000-square-foot open main floor that includes an oversized living/dining room, powder room, butler's pantry, kitchen, and large family room. An ornamental steel, glass, and wood stair leads you to the second floor, which includes two en-suite bedrooms and a large master bedroom. The lower level includes a large recreation room and additional bedroom, as well as a mud room that leads to a heated two-car garage. Interior finishes include wide oak hardwood floors and Italian cabinetry in the kitchen and bathrooms. Exterior features include a tiered rear deck with an overhead steel terrace and built-in planters over the garage, as well as a cantilevered balcony off the second floor master bedroom.

Kitchen cabinets modeled in SketchUp

Figure G12.2 Kitchen, wire frame.

Figure G12.3 Add textures, furniture, and other objects.

Figure G12.1 Front view.

Figure G12.4 Add lights and objects.

Figure G12.5 Lighting effects and reflections.

Figure G12.6 Colors.

Figure G12.7 Final kitchen rendered in SketchUp.

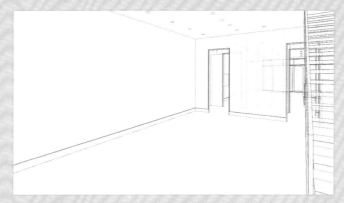

Figure G12.8 Wire frame of living/dining area.

Figure G12.9 Applying photo textures to the floor.

Figure G12.10 Importing 3D furniture and other objects.

Figure G12.11 Importing the scene into Maxwell Studio.

Figure G12.12 Final rendered scene with lights in SketchUp.

Figure G12.13 Wire frame of bathroom.

Figure G12.14 Applying photo textures to the floor and walls.

Figure G12.15 Importing 3D fixtures and other objects.

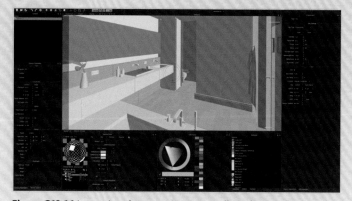

Figure G12.16 Importing the scene into Maxwell Studio.

Figure G12.17 Rendered scene with lights.

Figure G12.18 Final rendering in SketchUp.

Dunes House, Indiana Dunes by Patrick Rosen, Rosen Architecture

The special effect is fog. It softens the background, helps you focus on the model, and gives a feeling of depth to the environment. The default view angle is 35 degrees, but you can drag it up a few degrees to exaggerate the perspective. Once everything is modeled, export it into Photoshop, where you can adjust the brightness, contrast, and color saturation. (**Tip:** The Dune could be modeled with the **Sandbox** tools. Using the **Draw>Sandbox>From Scratch**, drag a grid with 10-foot square segments. Triple-click on the area. Then pull points on that area of grid upward to various heights based on the topographical survey.) Use the **Soften Edges** command and select the maximum amount of softening. Select the **Soften Coplanar Option** to remove any fractals. The trees are 2D SketchUp trees that were downloaded from an online site from Google Warehouse. (**Tip:** Although the 2D trees are flat, they orient themselves toward the viewer, as long as they are at ground level.) The 2D trees may work better than 3D because they are more realistic. 3D trees also take up a lot of memory and slow down the computer's ability to process the model. (**Tip:** For modifications in the sandbox tool, hold the arrow up or down on the keyboard while using the move tool. This will keep the move in the "Z" axis.)

Figure G12.20 Front View. Finished SketchUp rendering with shadows, landscape, and terrain. The vertical reverse board and batten siding was provided as a SketchUp material and downloaded from the manufacturer's (Certainteed) website. The concrete foundation wall material is a standard SketchUp material complete with form-tie marks and joints.

Figure G12.21 Interior View. Set camera at a 24mm wide angle, which is a good angle for viewing interiors of small rooms.

Figure G12.19 Front View. Freehand sketch over SketchUp rough model.

Chicago House, Lincoln Park by Patrick Rosen

Rendering Techniques: Similar graphic techniques to the Dunes House were used here, except that in the city environment, in order for the new house to stand out from the adjoining houses, modeled generic gray massing blocks were used to represent the existing houses. These were based on aerial images from Google Earth for the neighboring building footprints. Site photos were used to set the height of the modeled image. You can also use Google Earth street view for comparison.

Figure 12.22 Chicago House, Lincoln Park by Patrick Rosen.

CHAPTER 13

Multifamily Residential Design

Objectives

- Understand and become familiar with different multifamily types, including townhouses, apartments, and mixed-use buildings.
- Understand site access issues and the sequence of entries, from building entry to elevator lobby to corridor to apartment/townhouse entry.
- Understand why some apartments are narrow and others are wide and what are the advantages and disadvantages of each type.
- Learn how to compare multifamily housing to the previously studied single-family homes and how to design for both types.
- Understand new graphic techniques that integrate freehand and digital images in these residential types.
- Design a one-bedroom unit of about 425 square feet, using a new app for iPad called Home Design 3D.
- Learn how to construct a stairway using SketchUp tools.

Overview

What are the chief differences among these housing types? What are the comparable densities? This chapter shows how to use freehand sketching and SketchUp from concept sketches to finished models and then use Photoshop for finishing to demonstrate the multifamily housing type and its place in the community. Principles of design, as well as graphics, are explored.

Townhouses

This townhouse, based on a bungalow plan, can be designed for a lot sized from 25 feet to 37.5 feet in width. Grouping three of them together, they fit on a 75-foot lot. That can accommodate a garage at the rear (alley) yard, housing two cars each.

The key to understanding townhouse design is the shape and placement of the stairway. In SketchUp, we can create several different types of stairways: the straight run, the corner, and the switchback. (See Figures 13.3a to 13.3d.) We can easily construct these stairways in SketchUp by using guidelines on the plan to show the width of the stairs and treads. Then draw guidelines vertically, based on the riser height. (**Tip**: Create a group of one-half level of stairs and a landing. Combine this group with a second by elevating it and rotating it according to the plan. We have chosen a switchback stair for this townhouse. We have located it near, but not at, the entry to allow space for a foyer and coat closet.)

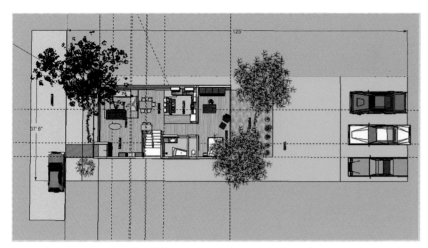

Figure 13.1 Site plan. Use SketchUp to convert a one-story bungalow to a two-story townhouse.

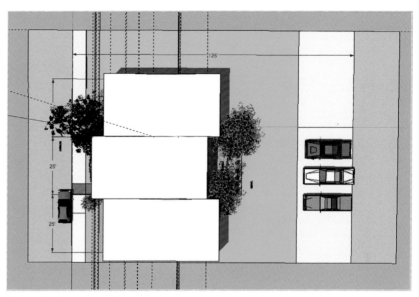

Figure 13.2 Site plan with staggered houses.

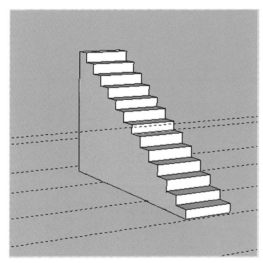

Figure 13.3a In a townhouse, the stairway is critical. It should be placed where it will not interfere with the main rooms, convenient to the entry, and central where it lands on the second floor. Here are three examples, starting with the straight stairway.

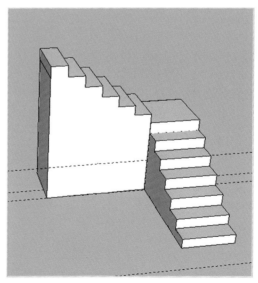

Figure 13.3b Corner stairway.

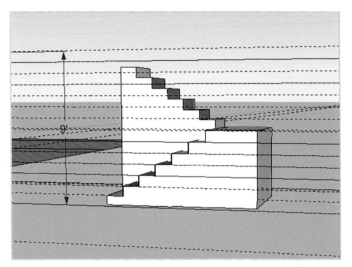

Figure 13.3c Switchback stairs. This was designed by laying out the number of risers with guidelines for the floor-to-floor space of 9 feet. Then a group was formed, copied, and flipped. Finally, a landing group was added.

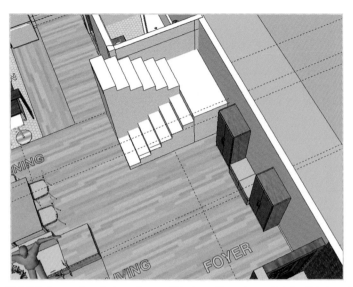

Figure 13.3d Stairway view in townhouse. We chose the scissor stair for this townhouse.

Save a screenshot of the first-floor plan and open it in Photoshop. Now we will create a rectangle for the second floor and turn down its opacity to about 20 to 30 percent so we can view the floor below. (See Figure 13.4a.) The stairway will be cut out to be clear. Use the rooms below to inform the rooms on the second floor, especially in the case of stackable plumbing. You can then turn off the layer showing the first floor for a clean view of the second-floor plan. You can also add notes and dimensions.

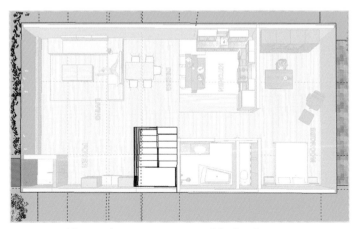

Figure 13.4a Second floor with a transparent view of the first floor to trace over. Trace on a separate Photoshop layer.

Figure 13.4b Second-floor plan. In Photoshop, add a layer of white below the floor plan and turn off the first-floor layer.

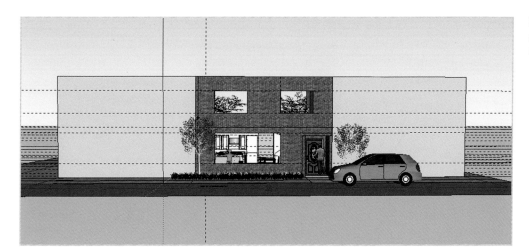

Figure 13.5 Façade of three townhouses.
Adjoining houses are shown in gray for massing only.

Figure 13.6 Façade of principal townhouse.

Let's turn our attention now to the façade. Render the middle townhouse for focus, while leaving the outer two gray. Add a car, landscaping, and a nice front door from components. Place a person entering as viewed from behind. (**Tip**: You can request "people from behind" as a search term from Google components. You can also add a "man walking a dog.")

Set the middle townhouse about 4 feet in front of the other two to add texture to the streetscape. (See Figure 13.2.) Now show different angles for the streetscape views and turn on **View>Shadows**. (See Figures 13.7 to 13.10.) Take some screenshots for your presentation.

Figure 13.7 Front view of townhouse from street.

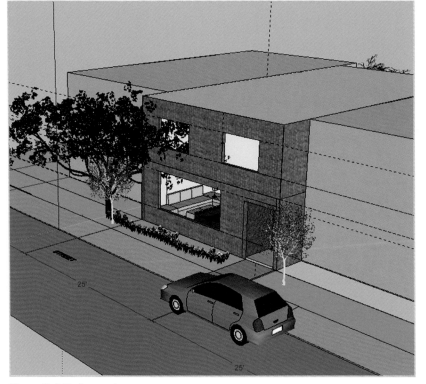

Figure 13.8 Bird's-eye view.

Figure 13.9 Front entry and streetscape with shadows and people.

Figure 13.10 Street view.

Deep Apartments (or Flats)

For reasons having to do with site plan and certain economies, some apartment footprints are deeper than optimal. This can result in a floor plan with fewer windows than is desirable in principal rooms. Some of the older apartment buildings, like six-flats for example, have stairways located between the apartment tiers, rather than at the rear. This creates through apartments, opening up views to the rear as well as the front.

You can place the second bedroom or a study at the rear. This layout also encourages cross-ventilation. Use the digital pen to sketch over the original floor plan. This time, draw in white and create a black background for your sketch.

In SketchUp, copy from previous saved files for kitchens and bathrooms and paste them into the new footprint. From here you can study different views of the deep apartment.

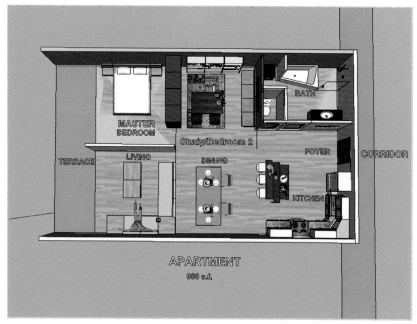

Figure 13.11 Deep apartment floor plan. SketchUp floor plan. Where lots are narrow, the result is often a deep plan. This is for a corridor-loaded building.

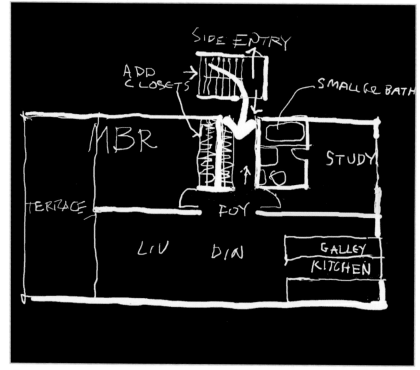

Figure 13.12 Sketch optional plan, side entry. (Drawing reversed, black background in freehand white sketching.) This drawing was sketched on a new layer over the SketchUp plan in Photoshop with the original layer hidden. It shows the advantage of a side entry with fenestration in the front and back rooms. This is also true of many small, walkup apartment buildings.

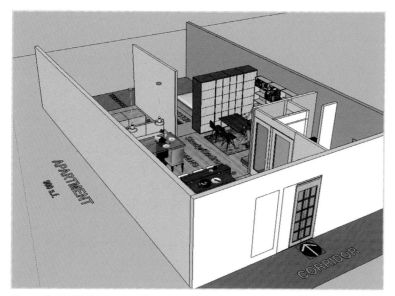

Figure 13.13a Bird's-eye view from entry.

Figure 13.13b Bird's-eye closeup from kitchen.

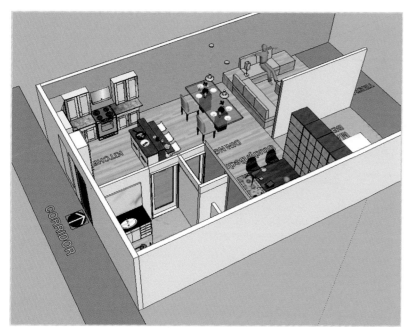

Figure 13.13c Cutaway bird's-eye view from entry corridor.

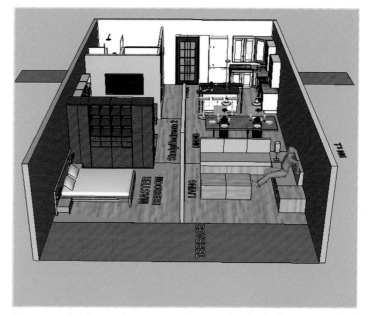

Figure 13.13d Cutaway view from front terrace, showing bedroom and living/dining room.

Wide Apartments

This type of apartment is usually found in moderate-height to tall elevator buildings with corridors, although it could also be designed for a three-story walkup with stairways in place of elevators.

The designer can accommodate a variety of apartment types based on a 30-foot structural grid. Place a studio, one-bedroom, and two-bedroom next to each other in the plan, as shown in Figure 13.15. Then furnish the two-bedroom unit with your favorite components. The split plan, dividing the two bedroom/bathroom suites with the central great room envisions a separation between family members or individual blended family groups. The great room can then be used for larger group activities, like cooking, eating, and watching TV. There is also an outdoor terrace across the front of the whole apartment. It is divided from adjoining units by wing walls for privacy and is set back from the façade for

protection from rain and sun. This increases the usefulness of the terrace during all seasons.

Bathroom suites are different in the two-bedroom suites. One bedroom is a master that has a large soaking tub and a separate water closet. This bedroom includes a desk, an armoire, and a bookcase. The second bedroom, envisioned for use by two students, whether related or not, includes a bath and shower in the suite, as well as a washer/dryer unit. It also includes a separate water closet. The beds in this room each have a night table and a lamp. They are subtly illuminated by **Photoshop>Filter>Rendering>Lighting Effect**. There are also two desks and chairs with lamps, as well as an armoire and a bookcase.

This apartment grouping of studios, one-bedroom, and two-bedroom units can be repeated in any combination and number the developer feels will best work for the buyer or rental market.

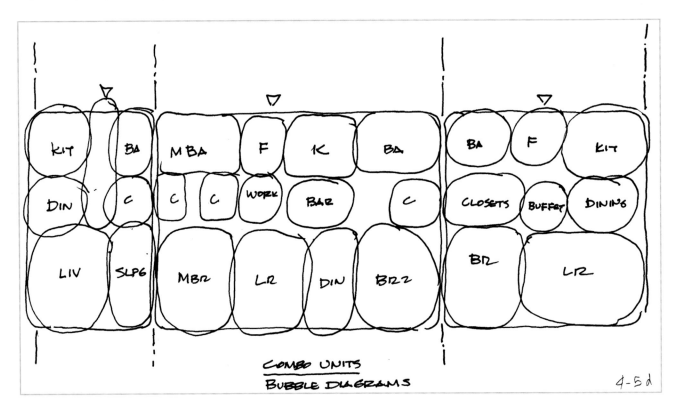

Figure 13.14 Apartment bubble diagram.

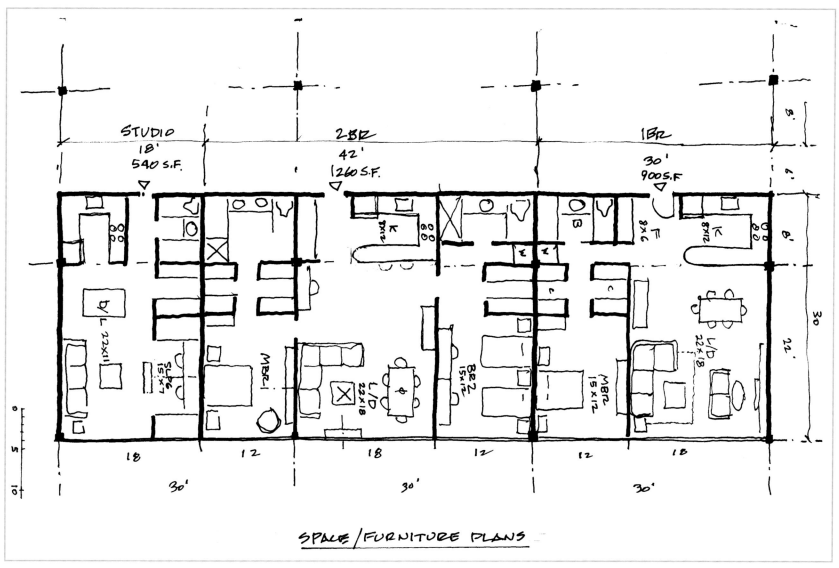

Figure 13.15 Apartment plans, space, and furniture sketch. Drawn freehand, these plans are often part of developer plans, where sufficient land is available to spread the building out. The wide front affords better light and views.

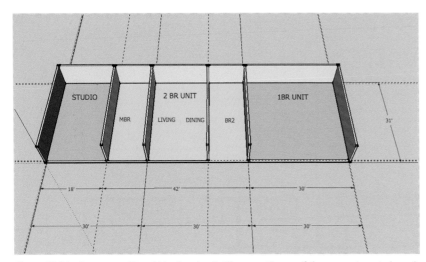

Figure 13.16a Convert to SketchUp drawing in Fig. 13.15. Group of three apartments based on a 30-foot structural grid. Mix of studio, one-bedroom, and two-bedroom units.

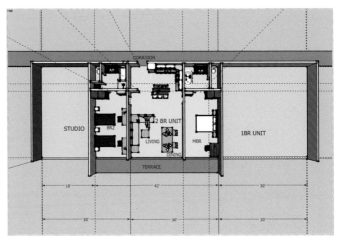

Figure 13.16b Unit group/plan with corridor and terrace. Showing two-bedroom unit split floor plan. Bedroom wings are separated for independent living suites.

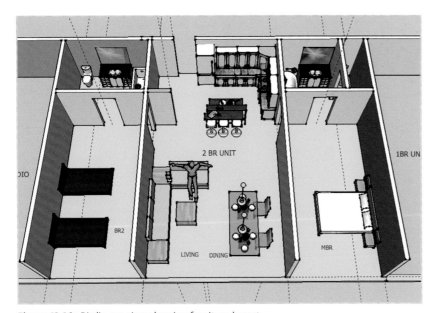

Figure 13.16c Bird's-eye view showing furniture layout.

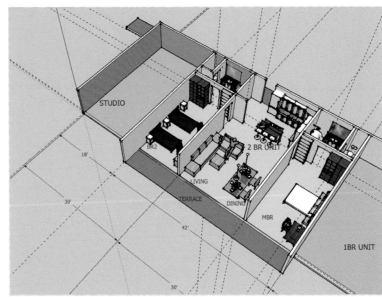

Figure 13.16d Bird's-eye oblique view.

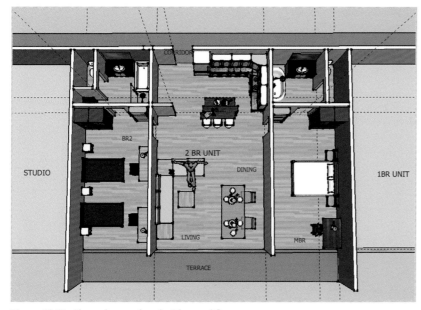

Figure 13.17a Floor plan rendered with wood floors.

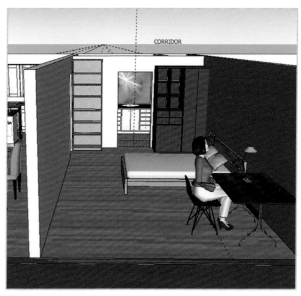

Figure 13.17b Master bedroom view. Furniture includes armoire, bookshelves, and desk/chair.

Figure 13.17c Living/dining/kitchen view.

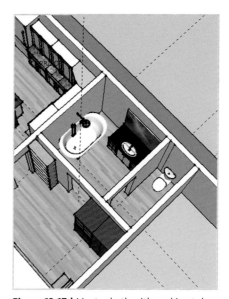

Figure 13.17d Master bath with soaking tub, large lavatory and mirror, and separate water closet room.

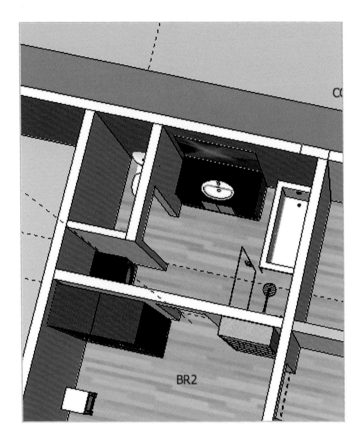

Figure 13.17e Bath 2 with washer/dryer space, a separate water closet room, and a separate shower.

Figure 13.17f Bedroom 2, meant to be shared by two students, includes desks, bookshelves, and night tables.

The Paris Flat

This apartment is based on tighter space requirements and a smaller structural bay. Historically, each bay in the unit has a large French casement window at one end. The rooms are about 10 feet wide, rather than the 12 feet we have previously planned. For this plan, we have used an app for iPad called Home Design 3D. It is much simpler than SketchUp but follows the same principles with a limited number of components.

The clients for this project are a couple of university French History professors who live in Paris three to six months per year for their research.

Each one requires a private workspace with a door between them. Office furniture includes a desk, chair, lamp, bookcase, and supply cabinet. There is a dresser for clothing on either side of the bed, with a reading lamp on each. There is a walk-in closet (with two armoires for hanging clothes), leading to a separate lavatory/bathroom. The water closet is separate and can be accessed by a door near the living room.

In the foyer there is a coat closet and three bookcases. The apartment includes a compact kitchen, a dining room table that can comfortably seat four people, and a small sectional sofa for lounging. With any luck, they will also have a terrace.

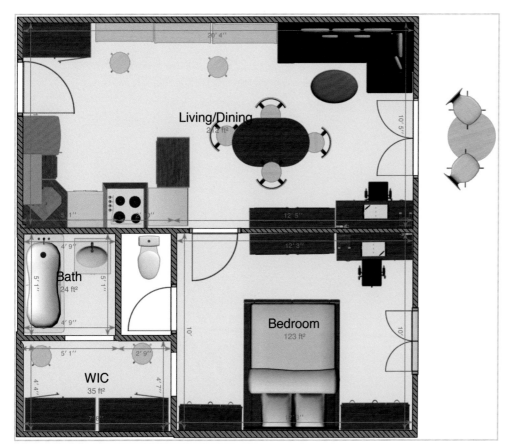

Figure 13.18 Floor Plan made with Home Design App for iPad. It's similar to SketchUp but much simpler to use. Paris is a very tight real estate market, so apartments are notably smaller than they are elsewhere. It was a challenge to design a one-bedroom unit for two people. Again, separating the toilet from the tub and washroom affords privacy. Each person has an armoire for clothes, a bookshelf, and a desk for work.

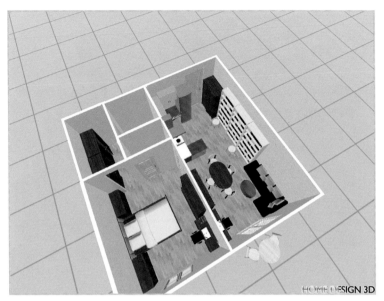

Figure 13.19a Bird's-eye view of bedroom/living room and terrace, roof hidden.

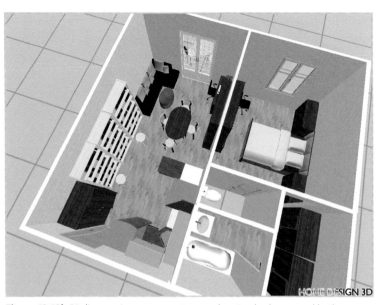

Figure 13.19b Bird's-eye view over great room showing bedroom and bath.

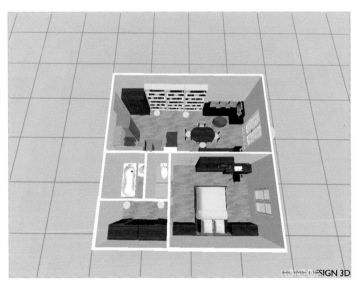

Figure 13.19c Bird's-eye view of bedroom and bathroom closet suite.
Shows how divided bathroom, closet armoires, and separate study areas can work to afford privacy for two people.

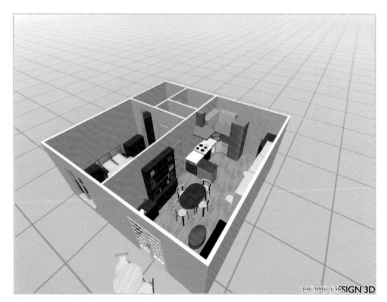

Figure 13.19d Bird's-eye view from terrace showing great room.

Mixed-Use Buildings: A Sustainable Building Type

Mixed-use buildings provide the best type of structure for sustainability of cities, particularly when they are of a relatively high density and located near public transportation. The density for a six-story building is approximately 92 dwellings per acre. There are several reasons to choose this building height and density. It avoids many of the pitfalls of very tall buildings, such as shadows cast, wind around the periphery, high parking requirements, and space needed between buildings to maintain light and air. Technically, the elevators required for this building height are not as expensive as for the taller elevator shafts. Perhaps the most important reason, however, is the footprint on the neighborhood. Going back to the example of Paris, the six-story building nestles nicely into neighborhoods even of lower buildings. It doesn't dominate. It's a good neighbor. And it provides services that are useful to everybody. The density of residential dwellings above the retail shops is a ready market for the stores and encourages them to locate there, which in turn encourages people to be on the street and creates a more secure environment. The more people who live near where they do their daily shopping, the less likely they are to drive. This cuts down drastically on air pollution and the potential for vehicular crashes.

However, with this density and traffic, some problems are unavoidable and must be mitigated. Street planting can help muffle the sound of cars. The need for outdoor space can be ameliorated by use of outdoor terraces for the apartments. Public transportation must use quiet technology, rubber wheels, and other things so that the noise level they produce is low. Cafés and bars can be located near tiers of the building that contain offices, rather than residences, so they aren't disturbed by noise at night. But for people who absolutely do not want to be located on a commercial street, there's always the other side of the building.

Another problem for mixed-use developments in the United States is financing. Due to out-of-date federal regulations for mixed-use buildings, they have very high capital requirements. The Congress for the New Urbanism is working with the Federal Government to fix this problem.[1]

The street right-of-way for Main Street is normally 100 feet (see Figures 13.20 and 14.7). This is wide enough to provide a spacious sidewalk area that can accommodate cafés and sidewalk markets. In the center, you can provide a platform and tracks for a light rail or streetcar system. Several tradeoffs must be made for any given community. Providing bike lanes on this street would take up part of the driving space. Permanent parking may have to be provided off the main street, inside the building, or in the rear of the building.

Outdoor space should be provided in the form of a terrace in front of the building. Planting on this terrace can also help ameliorate sound. Or residential units could be situated on higher floors.

The elements that most affect mixed-use development include the following:

- Size of roadway. Whether a main street or local street will determine the amount of setback necessary to protect a unit from noise and pollution.
- Availability of daily shopping.
- Public transportation. Availability of public transportation will affect the walkability and convenience of a neighborhood and may cut down on the necessity of daily automobile use, especially for short trips.
- Parking. If the density of the neighborhood is high, and there is no public transportation, it may be necessary to provide off-street parking. Will it be interior to the building or in a separate building?

---

1. Condos and apartments attached to retail are difficult to finance in the United States because of Federal Housing Authority (FHA), Fannie Mae, Freddie Mac, and Housing and Urban Development (HUD) 221d4 regulations. Multiple-unit rental capital programs have excessively tight restrictions that force developers to build high to qualify. See the Congress for the New Urbanism website (http://www.cnu.org/liveworkwalk), which explains how the FHA is slowly moving toward fixing this problem.

- Entertainment. Is there enough 24/7 (or at least 18/7) entertainment in the neighborhood? People going out at night creates a strong sense of security in a community.

SketchUp provides many good components for urban design scale, including light rail cars, trees, street lamps, café furniture, people, and automobiles. (**Tip:** Remember to turn the **View>Shadow** tool on to see where shadows will be cast in your model and at what time of day. Will there be sun on your favorite breakfast café in the morning? Also, you can use the **Lighting Effect** tool to show the effect of street lamps on a building or on the nighttime streetscape.)

This chapter also includes some examples of six-story mixed-use buildings in Paris. One shows the entry to the building through a street market.

Other questions will have to be answered to complete the interior design plan, such as the following:

- Workplaces. Is a community planned to allow living and working spaces to be within walking distance, or a short commute, of each other?
- Home office. If a resident works at home, there will be a need to plan space so as to not intrude into the resident's personal life.
- Walkability. If a community is walkable—say 10 minutes maximum walk for daily needs—there will be less need for parking, or certainly no need for second cars.
- Shopping. Grocery shopping in particular needs to be located nearby. Healthy foods are perishable. Fruits and vegetables should be sold on a daily basis, as is done in Europe. If shopping is convenient, it can be a pleasure rather than a chore.
- Storage. The more daily shopping is done, the less need there will be for storage in a home.

- Foyer. If a foyer opens directly to a public street, it will be necessary to plan it for security, as well as climate control, such as a closed entry or a mud room. If it opens from an apartment corridor, less space will be required for the foyer.
- View. If a view is unobstructed, the entire orientation of the home will probably be planned around it. If views are tight, or streets are narrow, there will be a greater need for privacy. This will affect window coverings, as well as room layouts. Interior lighting will be much more important.

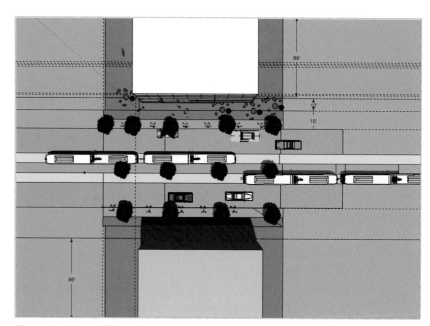

Figure 13.20 Overall Site. Mixed-use commercial and residential building on main commercial street with tram in center median. Use SketchUp to set up the site plan.

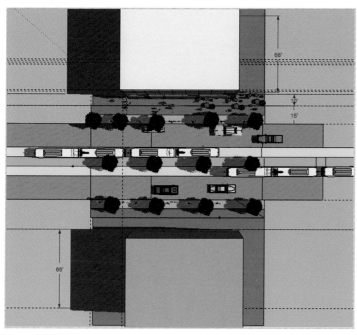

Figure 13.21 Site plan close up.

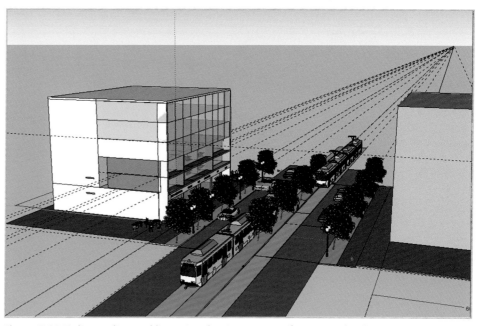

Figure 13.22 Bird's-eye, distant oblique view showing cutaway of apartment levels.

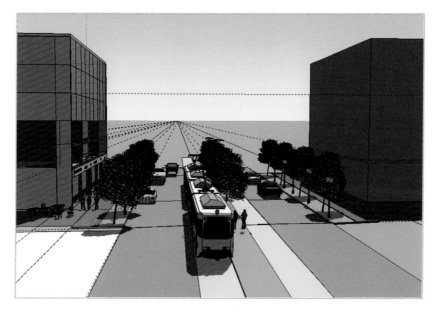

Figure 13.23 Bird's-eye view of tramway on median.

Figure 13.24a Bird's-eye oblique view showing streetscape.

Figure 13.24b Bird's-eye medium-distance view of streetscape and tramway near retail stores with shadows.

Figure 13.24c Closeup bird's-eye view of tramway and street.

Figure 13.25 Façade with tram in front.

Figure 13.26a Commercial/residential building with balconies above street and streetlights.

Figure 13.26b Commercial/residential building with balconies above street. Show illumination of streetlights with Photoshop, as described in Figures 6.11e and 6.11f, the art gallery project.

Figure 13.26c Streetscape in SketchUp.

Figure 13.26d Freehand version of streetscape showing greater detail. Traced over
SketchUp model. Rendered with markers and colored pencils.

Figure 13.26e Closeup bird's-eye view of balcony, storefront, sidewalk, and
streetlights.

**Figure 13.26f Balcony and streetscape closeup view with illuminated street
lighting.** Remember to use Filter>Render>Lighting Effects to illuminate street
lighting. (**Tip:** By now you may want to set up folders of your own images of people,
street scenes, furniture, and other entourages for use with future Photoshop
images.)

Figure 13.27 Paris mixed-use building with bakery at corner and apartments above.

Figure 13.28 Paris mixed-use building with flower shop at rounded corner and apartments above.

Figure 13.29 Paris mixed-use building with fish market, butcher, bakery, wine shop, cheese shop, charcuterie, and café at corner. Temporary farmers' market sets up three times per week on the public place.

Figure 13.30 Monoprix store at street level. Dormers on mansard roof at top floor.

Tools

- Using SketchUp, Copy, and Paste, we have studied three types of stairways for townhouses.
- We have used the translucent floor layer to trace a floor plan and show how it can be converted to a simple black-on-white drawing.
- We have used SketchUp to show different urban elements with mixed-use buildings.

KEY TERMS

Straight run stairway: A stairway that runs from floor to floor without a landing.

Corner stairway: A stairway that starts from one direction, then turns a right angle, and continues up.

Switchback stairway: A stairway that traverses up one-half level to a landing, then turns back, and continues to the second floor.

Tread: The width of a single stair from front to back.

Riser: The height from one tread vertically to the next. Usually an equal division between floor heights. Per code, not to exceed 8 inches per riser.

EXERCISES AND PRACTICE

1. Draw a landscape plan for balcony roof gardens of different sizes, ranging from 3 feet deep to 8 feet deep.
2. Take a photographic survey of mixed-use buildings in your community. Try to determine how successful a business is based on the number of residential stories above it.
3. Similar to locations studied in the previous chapter, see how mixed-use buildings score on Walking Score and how that affects their property values. Sources for Walking Scores are as follows:
   a. http://www.ipa.udel.edu/healthyDEtoolkit/walkability/ (Walkability Assessment Tool from the University of Delaware)
   b. http://www.walkscore.com/ (Walk Score)
4. Layout and plan different configurations for townhouse plans based on the room sizes studied in this chapter.
5. Try a larger module to see what the implications would be. In a large living room, for example, would the furniture placement be close enough for convivial conversation?
6. Show a mix of apartment buildings, townhouses, and single-family homes on one block. Be sure to turn on shadows to see how the taller buildings affect the lower ones and their yards. Place the taller buildings advantageously so their shadows don't affect the lower ones.

ART GALLERY

Pappageorge Haymes Andersonville Townhouses

Twenty-three contemporary, two-story rowhouses are sited in the northside neighborhood of Andersonville. The two-story format features 57-foot-long plans, which allow the main living space to take full advantage of large private yards. Concrete panels clad the elevations, which contain floor-to-ceiling windows. Plans vary from 15 feet to 18 feet to 20 feet wide, ranging from 1,700 square feet to 2,250 square feet. The main level has a 10-foot ceiling height.

Figure G13.2 Wire frame perspective of kitchen/dining room.

Figure G13.1 View of townhouses and backyard gardens.

Figure G13.3 Applying photo textures and values to the kitchen cabinets and floor.

Figure G13.4 Importing 3D furniture and other objects.

Figure G13.5 Adding exterior landscaping.

Figure G13.6 Rendered scene with lights. Use Filter>Render>Lighting Effects for lamps.

Figure G13.7 Final rendering.

Pappageorge Haymes Mixed-Use Developments

The Bridgeport

This block-long, mixed-use development is found at the center of the Bridgeport neighborhood in Chicago. This large structure maintains a comfortable human scale. Retail parking is hidden behind the building but obviously accessed by pedestrians through a large vaulted passage flanked by shops. The ground perimeter is fully active, with retail in combination with a substantial residential density above.

Division and Clybourn

The architectural vision for this six-story structure responsibly gestures to immediate context, both traditional masonry buildings on Chicago's Division Street and North Clybourn Avenue, and the minimalist, industrial character of the Lakefront Mercy single-room occupancy (SRO) building. The plan holds the street edge of both Clybourn and Division, yet offers a setback to effectively widen the narrow sidewalks, leading to a generous, usable plaza. One of the projections drops to grade to signal the residential entry on Division Street.

Figure G13.8 Street view rendering.

Figure G13.9 Rendering from street.

Figure G13.10 Street view of a mixed-use center with sidewalk café.

The Ellington

Located in Detroit's Cultural Arts District, the 300-foot-long mixed-use building anchors the corner frontage along historic Woodward Avenue. The mixed-use condominium building represents the second phase of a 4.5-acre planned development that includes a six-story parking structure with 1,000 parking spaces, serving both the development and the surrounding neighborhood.

Figure G13.12 Street view 2.

Figure G13.11 Street view 1.

Jean-Paul Viguier: Mixed-Use Project in Metz, France

This project includes 80,000 square meters, incorporating shops, offices, and homes in mixed-use buildings. The blending of functions will create a more bustling and lively city and reduce the use discrepancies between peak and off-peak times. This project is located near the train station and Pompidou Centre. It forms part of a human-centric vision of the city, with multiple uses during days.

Figure G13.13 Street view, mixed-use center.

Figure G13.15 View of place and people.

Figure G13.14 Mixed-use place at night. Cultural center and mixed-use commercial/residential center.

Figure G13.17 Offices above atrium.

Figure G13.16 Interior entry lobby of shopping center with atrium and curving stairways.

Figure G13.18 Reception area at ground level.

PART IV

Site and Landscape Context: Community, Residential, and Commerce

In Part III, we covered a lot of ground. We've shown you how to think of integrated drawing techniques as part of the design process. In Part IV, we discuss how the site and context affect the residential interior and what factors constitute a community (**Chapter 14**). Then we plan a case study of a new community mixed-use building based on transportation-oriented design in the Humboldt Park area in Chicago. We will show how SketchUp and Photoshop can also be used to create urban plan schematics in a real community. You will also become familiar with Google Earth tools and importing SketchUp models into Google Earth (**Chapter 15**).

The Site and Landscape

The street determines the block; the block determines the lot; the lot determines the project orientation and design. And that all has a strong impact on the sequence and access to the residential interior.

Objectives

- Use the tools learned in Parts I, II, and III to demonstrate how the landscape and streetscape affect the site and the residential unit.
- Learn to load landscape components from SketchUp, such as trees, shrubs, flowers, people, cars, and transit vehicles.
- Learn how to use photographs of the landscape, streetscape, and people to make collages with the models they design.
- Understand the relationship between the street, the site, and the design project.

Overview

Residence access is a result of lot layout. The essential character of residential design is directly related to the way you enter the unit and the streetscape. A rich and active street life can result in a secure and interesting entry sequence. A quiet, landscaped street can produce a calm, peaceful ambience for the home. This is a choice for clients.

This chapter shows how you can plan a variety of home sites and home entry sequences based on different lot subdivisions. These can result in various densities, as well as mixed heights. There is obviously a greater opportunity for landscaping in suburban or edge city areas, because of the larger open space. The challenge remains to bring the landscape into higher-density urban areas. We'll show how the drawing and digital techniques demonstrated in this book will help students and professionals visualize an integration of the landscape into all aspects of the built environment. This includes the view from windows, interior and balcony planting, and the streetscape.

Site Considerations

Long before you enter your home, many design principles have been established. Questions such as the following must be answered:

1. Are there views to enjoy?
2. Is there privacy?
3. Is the entry protected from the weather?
4. Is there traffic to screen out?
5. Is it a walkable community?
6. Is a car necessary, and is one enough?

These factors are all predetermined by the site context and the specific streetscape.

An Active and Attractive Street

There are many different kinds of streets and approaches to a residential community, ranging from low-density single-family communities to high-density apartment and mixed-use urban communities. They all have advantages and shortcomings. It will ultimately be up to the client to determine the location of the site, but economic considerations, safety, transportation, and other factors all affect this choice. The designer should be familiar with these considerations to better advise his or her client.

State Street, Chicago, has earned fame from the song lyrics "State Street, that great street." The latest renovation of State Street has sparked a new wave of residential development in the formerly abandoned offices located above the street-level stores.

New York has also initiated a series of street transformations that have made the city more conducive to 24-hour residential, entertainment, and commercial life.

Figure 14.2 Manhattan shared-space street, showing cars, cyclists, and sidewalk cafés.

Figure 14.1 State Street, "That Great Street," Chicago. Historic District; Carson, Pirie, Scott and Company store (designed by Louis Sullivan).

San Francisco has created several parklets in the street rights-of-way to calm traffic and provide additional space for recreation.

Paris streets are the primary models for mixed-use residential and commercial use. Although the buildings are not particularly tall, approximately six stories, they are fairly high in density and therefore accommodate a very active and rich street life. Traffic must be controlled for the improvement of the quality of residential life above the ground-level retail.

Streets that are only residential can also be very attractive and lavishly landscaped, and that would be a choice for some clients. Even these residential streets can be close to commercial facilities if they are planned correctly.

Figure 14.3 San Francisco parklet occupying a portion of the street.

Figure 14.4 Paris street scene, apartments above market.

Figure 14.5 Paris, with high-density residential above stores.

Figure 14.6 Residential streetscape, Chicago.

Types of Streets and Lots

Main Street is the lifeline for most communities, whether they are high or low density. Typically, it is a wide street, with about 100-feet right-of-way. Ideally, it should have a boulevard character, with a landscaped median and wide sidewalks for cafés and landscaping. The median allows for a pedestrian refuge when crossing the street, and it also provides greater safety for traffic. When possible, protected bike lanes should be provided as well. The Institute of Transportation Engineers determines street standards.[1] Engineers now are much more cognizant of the importance of developing standards for "complete streets," which include walkability, traffic calming, streetscape use, and landscaping, rather than traffic-only solutions.

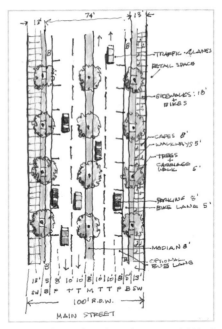

Figure 14.7 Main Street. Typical mixed residential/commercial block, with a 100-foot right-of-way, 8-foot center median and left turn lane, 13-foot sidewalk and café space, 5-foot bike lanes, heavy to moderate traffic, and able to accommodate a public transit lane.

---

1. The Institute of Transportation Engineers, "Context-Sensitive Solutions in Designing Major Urban Thoroughfares for Walkable Communities" (Washington, DC: Author, 2006). Under the auspices of the Federal Highway Administration and the Congress for the New Urbanism.

Secondary streets are narrower; typically they have a right-of-way width of about 60 feet. They can have multiple uses, for light retail stores, mixed-use buildings, or residential only. Secondary streets are quieter and have less traffic than main streets. Ideally, secondary streets are within a short walking distance of main streets. They are feeders to a Main Street where one would find shops and businesses. Secondary streets can allow bicycles, but they are usually with shared lanes.

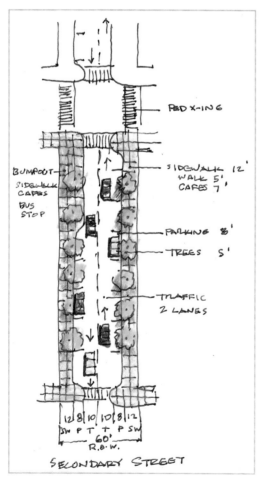

Figure 14.8 Secondary Street. Typical city or suburban street. Can have commercial mix or just residential, with moderate to light traffic.

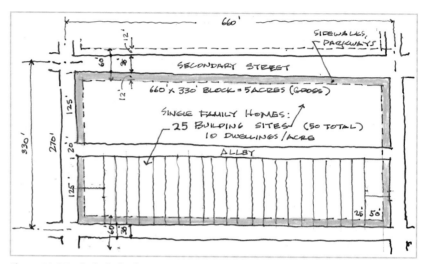

Figure 14.9 Typical Block Plan. Has 330 feet by 660 feet centerline dimensions and 5 acres gross area. Shown with alley in back and standard arrangement of long narrow lots, with square lots at corners.

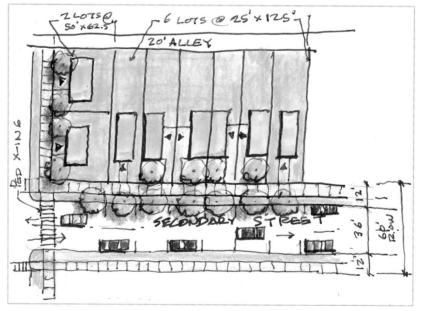

Figure 14.10 Homesites. This plan shows the various types of homesites for a typical low-density neighborhood on a secondary street. Compare the side entries and front entries.

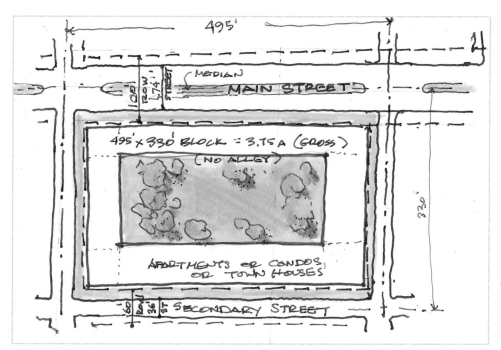

Figure 14.11 Short Block. Shorter blocks allow more paths for pedestrians and can ease traffic volumes. This plan shows no alley, so separate accommodations must be made for trash collection and delivery. Sometimes this is done through the front and sometimes through a courtyard entrance. It will affect the entry to the residences.

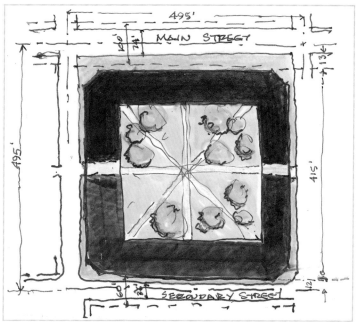

Figure 14.12 Square Block. Same plan only smaller. This size is similar to the block sizes in Paris and San Francisco. It creates a dense urban plan. Entry is through the front.

It should be noted that in hilly communities, the streets follow irregular patterns, weaving curves and angles into the natural landscape. Cities like Paris, San Francisco, and New York have hilly areas where the street patterns are more like spiderwebs than grids. We will show home designs on these hilly sites as well, using the SketchUp Sandbox Tool and Google Earth Terrain.

KEY TERMS

Module: A standardized unit of measurement.

Main street: The principal commercial street in a community, carrying a relatively heavy load of traffic.

Secondary street: The smaller collector streets that carry moderate-to light-weight volumes of traffic.

EXERCISES AND PRACTICE

1. Subdivide the five-acre block in a variety of ways for single-family homes. Use the alleys for parking or interior walkways.
2. Sketch a few different-sized blocks for other options. Smaller blocks create more streets and walking opportunities. These are found in higher-density communities.
3. Try a diagrammatic plan for an apartment building on one or more of these blocks shown. It can be any height you wish.
4. Show landscape plans for these different site configurations. How do site plans and streetscapes incorporate the landscape?
5. If you have Google SketchUp Pro, examine different hilly communities and explore the Terrain tool.

ART GALLERY

The following is an example of terrain modeling instructions with Google SketchUp Pro for accuracy in depicting hilly sites (Courtesy of Patrick Rosen Architect). Open SketchUp Pro, import Google Earth to SketchUp (for SketchUp Pro), and make terrain.

Figure G14.1 Step 1. Add a location in Geo-Locations: "Death Valley" California has been chosen here.

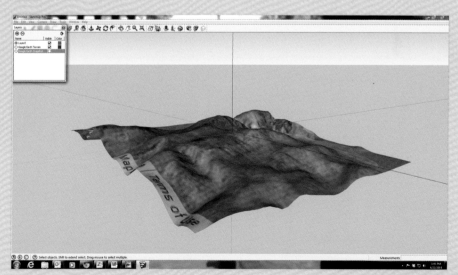

Figure G14.2 Step 2. Import map to SketchUp Pro using bent map icon.

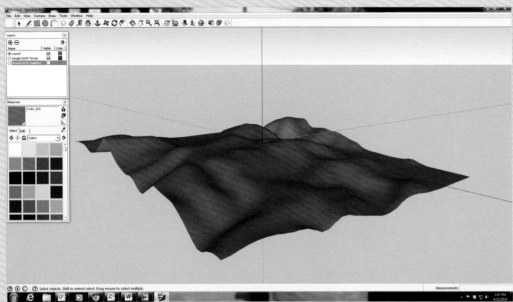

Figure G14.3 Step 3. Select Windows>Layers>. Uncheck the Google Earth snapshot visible option and check the box that makes Google Earth terrain visible. Uncheck Snapshot and select Terrain.

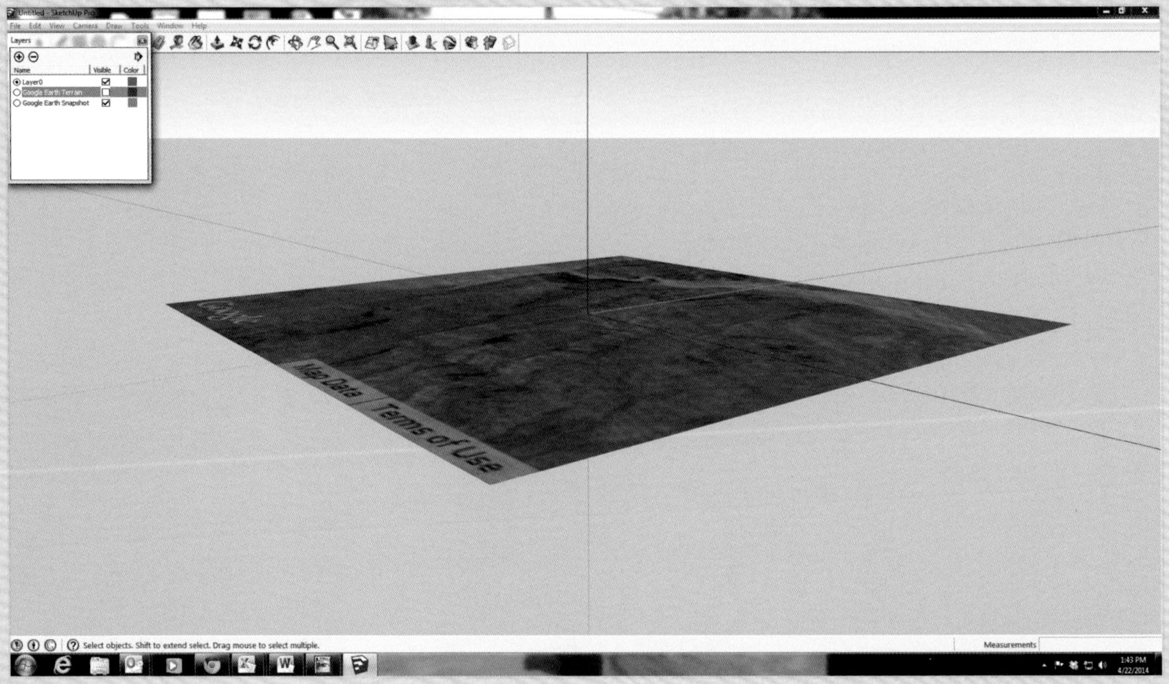

Figure G14.4 Step 4. You can then right-click, scroll to Edit Group, and with the Materials window, make it a gray color.

Placing Buildings in the Environment

Objectives

- Apply the mixed-use building prototype studied in **Chapter 13**, and place it in the context of the real-life community of Humboldt Park/West Town, Chicago.
- Use the technique of mass modeling in SketchUp to study the volume of the buildings.
- Understand the relationship between the mixed-use buildings and the community into which they will be placed**.**
- Learn techniques of importing SketchUp models into Google Earth so that they can show the buildings in their virtual environment.
- Learn how to adjust images with Photoshop and use freehand sketching over Photoshop models for presentations.
- Understand the relationship between the new buildings proposed for Main Street and the adjoining residential areas.

Overview

This chapter is a little different from the preceding chapters. We will apply freehand sketching, SketchUp modeling, and Photoshop finishing to a specific case study at a larger scale than before. We will also be very aware of a fourth technique here: analytical thinking. We need it to identify a relevant case study and to justify the subsequent choices we make in our work.

Case Study: Humboldt Park Mixed-Use Community Center

Reasons for Choosing This Site

Parts of the surrounding community of Humboldt Park have fallen into disrepair and underuse. Yet it is well located in the city and showing signs of spontaneous regeneration. We assert that a new and vital mixed-use residential/commercial building located in the community adjoining Humboldt Park would assist the spontaneous growth already underway and make the community a much more lively and walkable place. The study area contains approximately one square mile, or 640 acres.

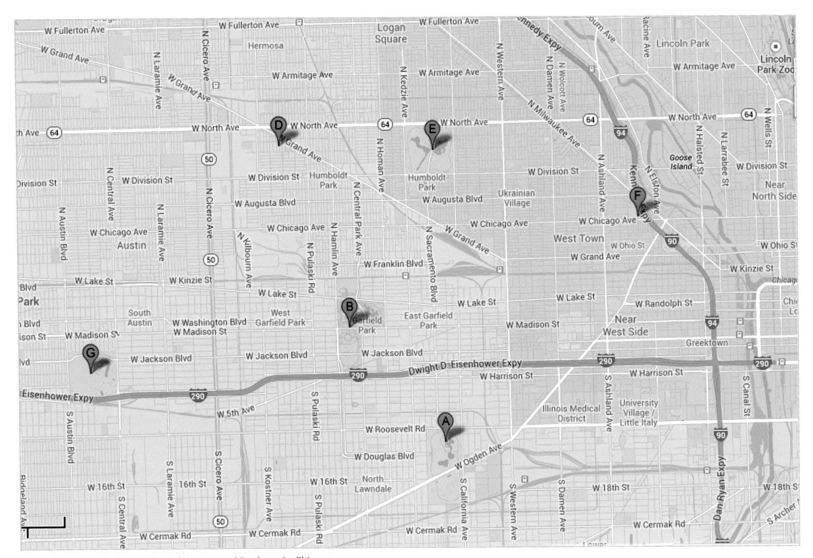

Figure 15.1 Map: The West Side Park System and Boulevards, Chicago.

In 1871, plans were completed for the entire ensemble by architect William Le baron Jenny, inspired by Frederick Law Olmsted. Jenny envisioned a series of parks with interlinking boulevards. In 1885, Jens Jensen, "dean of the Prairie Style landscape architecture," began working on the parks. The result has been one of the most historically important park systems in the United States.[1]

Following are examples of maps, Google Earth images, and 3D SketchUp modeling combined to aid the planning process for developing a mixed-use development north of Humbolt Park.

- The Boundaries are Bloomingdale to the North, Rockwell to the East, Augusta to the South, and Kimball to the West.
- Average population density in Humboldt Park, West Town communities is approximately 18,000 people per square mile. (Compared to approximately 11,919 per square mile overall in Chicago.)[2]

Figure 15.2 Gateway Statue across Division Street.

Figure 15.3 Street view on North Avenue, looking west.

1. Chicago Park District Website: http://www.chicagoparkdistrict.com/history/ city-in-a-garden/west-park-system/

2. Ibid.

Community Center

We have selected the focus of this site to be the intersection of Humboldt Boulevard and North Avenue for a community center, because it is the main connecting link from the community to the park. For this community center, a retail and entertainment building, we will develop the design for the Humboldt Café and the Humboldt Park Cinema, two main community attractions. First, make some freehand sketches of the site area from above and at eye level, as in Figures 15.4a–d.

Figure 15.4a Freehand Sketch of North Avenue and Humboldt Boulevard. Between Humboldt and Kedzie there are three streets intersecting with North Ave, and between Humboldt and California there are also three intersecting streets. In order to maintain the street pattern, it's necessary to break the mass into four buildings on each side of Humboldt Boulevard, or eight total.

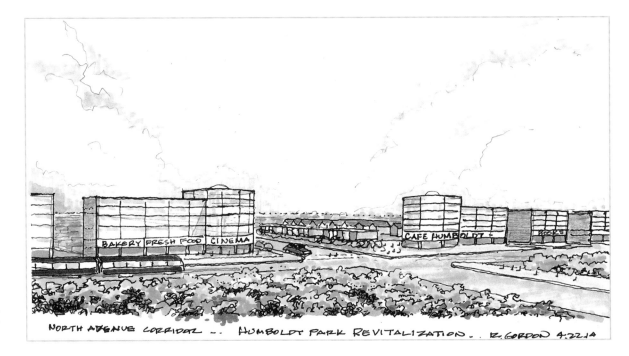

Figure 15.4b Humboldt Park Gateway. Use the SketchUp model as a basis for the sketch.

Figure 15.4c Bird's-eye view of Humboldt Park Gateway, pen and ink sketch.

Figure 15.4d Bird's-eye view of Humboldt Park Gateway, color rendering with markers and colored pencils.

Goals for a Community Center

- Identifying a community center would provide a focus to attract people.
- A café and cinema would anchor the community center and revitalize the street.
- A grocery store and bakery would provide fresh foods for the residents.
- People living in apartments overlooking Humboldt Park would have dramatic views of the park and downtown Chicago. The entire community would benefit from the increased activity and retail provisions.
- A shuttle bus or Bus Rapid Transit would provide needed public transportation on North Avenue and relieve some of the automobile congestion.
- Clear demarcation of the crosswalks into Humboldt Park serves to calm traffic and create a quiet, safe pedestrian ambience. Planted medians in the center of North Avenue will help create a boulevard atmosphere on the street and make it quieter and safer to cross. The extension of trees on Humboldt Boulevard helps integrate this urban center with the community.
- It would be a transit-oriented development, so that access to downtown would be easier.

Massing Models for Planning Context

You can then begin drawing a massing model in SketchUp. First, a mid-rise, mixed-use building for the North avenue blocks overlooking Humboldt Park. North Avenue is a major street, with public transportation. A high-density/mixed-use project transit-oriented design is appropriate here, but because it faces a park, we are limiting it to six stories in height. Also, we want the existing street network to remain connected so the masses necessarily open to the streets. See massing model (Figure 15.5) and street map (Figure 15.6).

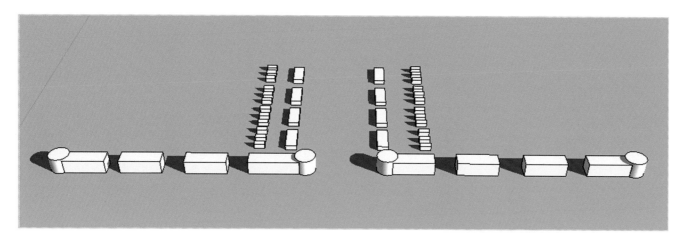

Figure 15.5 Looking north on Humboldt Boulevard, which leads into the park, make a simple massing model showing a midrise on North Avenue facing the park and low-rise housing and townhouses along Humboldt Boulevard with bungalows on the local streets behind.

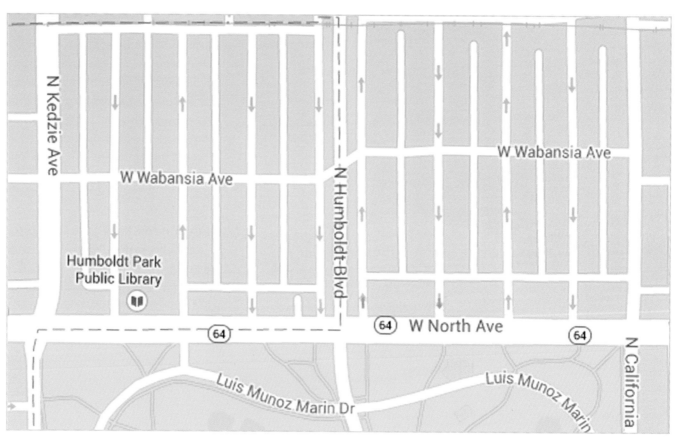

Figure 15.6 Map of Humboldt Park Retail Street, North Avenue. Shows the connection of local feeder streets.

Massing Models for the Case Study

Before making a finished architectural design, we want to get a general idea of the volume of a building and its placement in the community. A *massing model* is a conceptual design model meant only to show the volume of the building, rather than refined architectural design. In this case study, students will first produce a massing model of a mixed-use retail/residential/office development bordering on North Avenue, the north edge of Humboldt Park. (Use existing examples of mixed-use buildings as guides to the size you wish to propose.) The SketchUp models at this scale may appear oversimplified, but that's because they are massing models rather than refined architectural design. (Later, students will learn how to adjust the design, add details, and create a café, cinema, grocery store, street life, and public transportation in the plans.)

Figures 15.7 and 15.8 show how to import the massing model into Google Earth. Figures 15.9 to 15.22 show a 3D SketchUp massing model superimposed on the site with different view angles. Figures 15.23 to 5.34 show different close-up views of the community center in SketchUp. Figures 15.35 to 15.42 show freehand renderings of the buildings adding greater detail.

The Presentation: Community Outreach

The student has now successfully created a brand-new model for an existing community. Working in liaison with local community organizations, designers can play an active role in affecting the final plan for overall community improvement. By using the presentation tools in this book, the student or professional can now show a reasonable likeness of what the people are discussing. As in all work involving communities, this is just the start. Community meetings can be frustrating and even angering, but by providing the visual tools, the professional can provoke discussion and hopefully help bring the community into consensus. That's how communities are improved.

A Note on Historic Importance: Humboldt Park and the West Park System, Chicago (see Figure 15.6)

This historically important park system and community was influenced by some of the greatest architects, engineers, and landscape architects of their time: William le Baron Jenny, Fredrick Law Olmsted, and Jens Jensen. It was a response to a great need to provide recreational space and landscape to an underserved community, far from Chicago's lakefront parks and beaches.[3]

Current cultural, development, and planning practices are sensitive to historical material in communities. People often want the history of their place to be represented in any future plans. This could be simply through historic markers, restoration of important historic buildings, or walking and shopping patterns. It is important to know these concerns before meeting with the community.

Techniques for Importing SketchUp Models into Google Earth

The student will then import this model from Figure 15.7 into Google Earth (per the following directions) to show how it looks in context. As in other Google Earth views, we can also move it around for different views of our new model. Figures 15.9 to 15.12 are examples of maps, Google Earth images, and site-level photographs. Figures 15.13 to 15.22 show how SktechUp modeling can be combined with Google Earth to help visualize the buildings in the environment and aid the planning process. (Figures G15.1–G15.8 show how SketchUp and Photoshop can be combined as a basis for freehand conceptual sketches of existing buildings and proposed new buildings on the same sites.)

Now that students have completed their models in SketchUp, they can import them into Google Earth to see how they would look in the real or virtual world. First, the student will study the area with Google Maps and use Google Earth to "flyover" the community, using bird's-eye views and then street-level photos. Once familiar with the area, students can create their own models of buildings they think would be appropriate for the project and export them to Google Earth. It will take a little manipulating and adjustment, but the results are very satisfying and useful to the designer and the client as well.

---

3. Humboldt Park Census Data, Chicago: http://www.city-data.com/neighborhood/ Humboldt-Park-Chicago-IL.html; West Town Census Data, Chicago: U.S. Census, Record Information Services

Step-by-step approach

Follow the step-by-step approach associated with the images. Students should take these steps to achieve placement of models into Google Earth environments:

1. Open SketchUp
   a. Create a model or open an existing one.
   b. Remove "blips" for a clear image. **Window>Styles>Edit>** Remove checks from all boxes.
   c. Add **Geo Location** in SketchUp (**File>Geo-Location>Add Location**) or arrow on icon from toolbar.
   d. File>Export>3d model (name it) as a **COLLADA .dae** (Google Earth file) to desktop. This is very important.
2. Open Google Earth
   a. Locate the area where your model will be placed. Approximate is okay.
   b. Open the dae file you saved to the desktop from SketchUp.
   c. Options in Google Earth: Turn on 3D buildings (photorealistic)
   d. The open dae file will appear near your site on Google Earth.
   e. By gripping in the "ticked" area, you can move the model until it exactly lines up with your site.

   f. You can also stretch or rotate the model by using different grips on the green outline. This takes some getting used to, but it's worth it.
   g. Then click "OK" on the dialogue box to affix it to your Google Earth location.
   h. Save the image to your desktop. This will give you a screenshot in jpeg format that can be used in Photoshop.
3. Open Photoshop. **Tip:** Shadow settings are tied to geographical locations. On the default screen, the solid green line runs north, the dotted green south, and the dotted red line west.
   a. Save the image as a Photoshop (psd) file with appropriate resolution (72 ppi for screen use, 200 to 300 dpi for print use, depending on size of print).
   b. You can adjust the contrast, color, and other functions of Photoshop previously discussed in this book.
   c. You can also add layers for background, context, and style.
   d. Then save the image as a jpeg for future use. Jpeg will *flatten* the image and eliminate the layers.
   e. Keep the Photoshop image with the layers in case you want to change something later.

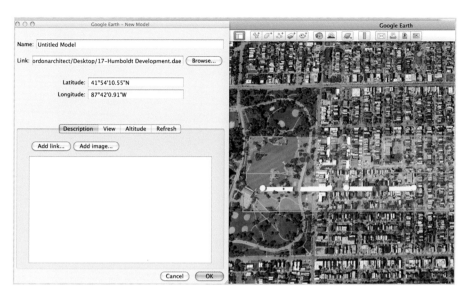

Figure 15.7 Set Geo-Location on SketchUp. File>Geo-Location>Add Location. Export model with name as a Collada File, .dae. (More details in text.) Open Google Earth. Find the approximate area where you will locate your model. Open the dae file you saved from SketchUp.

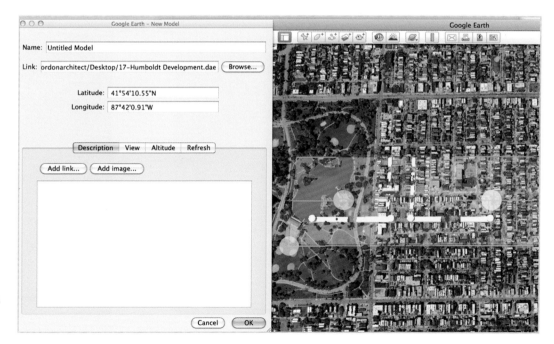

Figure 15.8 You will see your model in Google Earth. You can move it, stretch it, and rotate it with the grips outlined with yellow circles.

Figure 15.9 Bird's-eye view of Humboldt Park.

Figure 15.10 North edge of park, North Avenue.

Figure 15.11 Corner bird's-eye view of North and California.

Figure 15.12 Closeup view of North and California.

Figure 15.13 Bird's-eye view of North Avenue showing new development in place.

Figure 15.14 Zooming in, looking at harbor and park with development.

Figure 15.15 View your model in the context of its environment, the north edge of Humboldt Park, looking north.

Figure 15.16 Zoom in on the gateway leading to Humboldt Boulevard.

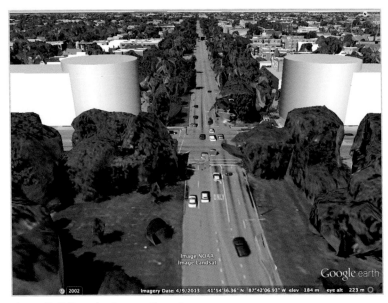

Figure 15.17 Zoom in closer on the gateway.

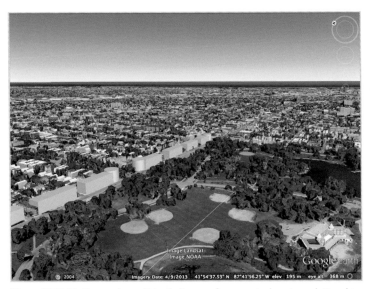

Figure 15.18 Bird's-eye view of North Avenue from west, showing relationship of new development to the park and surrounding community.

Figure 15.19 Oblique view of gateway from west.

Figure 15.20 Midrange bird's-eye view from the northeast corner of the park.

Figure 15.21 View of North Avenue with park, looking west.

Figure 15.22 Looking from inside the community south to the park.

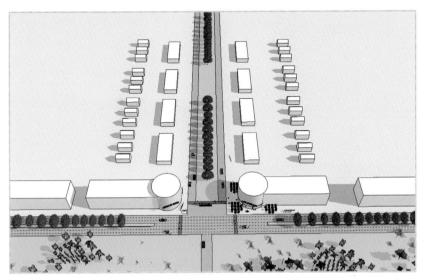

Figure 15.23 Massing model in SketchUp. Humboldt Park bird's-eye view, looking north on Humboldt Boulevard with North Avenue in the foreground.

Figure 15.24 Humboldt Boulevard, low bird's-eye view.

Figure 15.25 Café Humboldt, low angle.

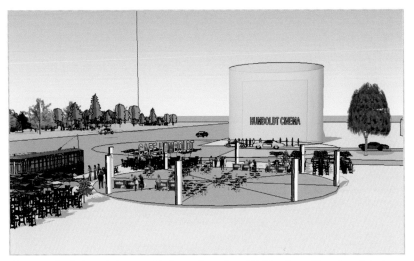

Figure 15.26 Café and cinema with the walls and roof hidden for café to show interior seating.

Figure 15.27 Café, North Avenue to East, showing crosswalk and median strip.

Figure 15.28 Pedestrian crossings at North and Humboldt.

Figure 15.29 Café corner, from park.

Figure 15.30 Cinema, streetcar, and park.

Figure 15.31 Bird's-eye view from the community, looking toward Humboldt Park.

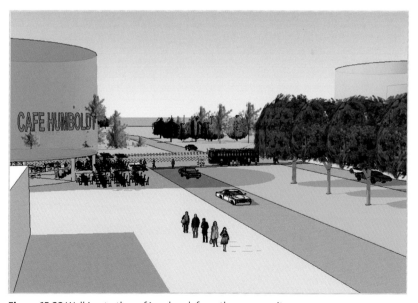

Figure 15.32 Walking to the café and park from the community.

Figure 15.33 View of the café through the trees on boulevard.

Figure 15.34 Humboldt Café, looking to cinema and streetcar stop, and Humboldt Park.

KEY TERMS

Flyover: Using a series of bird's-eye photographs, or screenshots, to give the impression of flying over a specific area. An advanced use of this technique would allow for animation videos.

Bus rapid transit: A hybrid public transportation system that borrows some elements of light rail, such as dedicated lanes, sheltered stations, ticket kiosks, and limited stops. It is far less expensive to build than light rail, however, and serves many public transit needs.

Massing model: A conceptual design model, meant only to show the volume of the building, rather than refined architectural design.

Transit-oriented development: A middle- to high-density residential and/or commercial building designed to place as many people as possible within short walking distance to transit.

Community collaboration: The process of using charettes (group meetings with graphic tools) to gather community opinion on design and planning issues.

EXERCISES AND PRACTICE

1. Attend community meetings to determine what the issues are that affect the people in a given community and write a report. This will be the basis for your project.
2. Create some SketchUp models you would like to see on a variety of sites in one or more communities.
3. Prepare a PowerPoint or slide presentation of what you might present to a community. Present it to your class for feedback.
4. Practice your verbal presentation style as well.
5. Select one project and develop it with more detail by freehand sketching over the massing model.
6. Try other uses of Google Earth: Take Field Notes with Google Earth images on an iPad or your computer.
7. You are now ready to explore other cities and sites. You can use Google Earth to search for sites of interest to you in your own town and take Field Notes right on the image. Use the digital pen or an iPad app for the notes.

(See the Art Gallery in **Chapter 13** for mixed-use developments by Jean-Paul Viguier, Pappageorge Haymes, and in Chicago.)

ART GALLERY

The following are street photos and colored freehand renderings of possible new, remodeled mixed-use buildings on North Avenue, making the street walkable.

Figure G15.1 Existing Humboldt Boulevard and North Avenue site.

Figure G15.2 Freehand rendering over photo showing possible new cinema building at Humboldt and North Avenue.

Figure G15.3 Gas station breaks street walking continuity. Replace it with active street enterprise like café, grocery, or hardware store.

Figure G15.4 New grocery store at North and Kedzie. Provide median planters and clear pedestrian crosswalks to the park.

Figure G15.5 Existing drive-in fast food on North Avenue.

Figure G15.6 Replace drive-in fast food with walk-in restaurant for street continuity. Parking can be provided at rear of site, not on North Avenue. Could be the same owner.

Figure G15.7 Existing new mixed-use building on North Avenue.

Figure G15.8 Freehand sketch of building in Figure G15.7. This type of new construction can be built as infill on vacant lots. It is consistent with the scale and mixed-use character of the street.

A Brief History of Computer-Aided Design

Some Background Notes

In the past, the architect/designer faced a choice as to how to start the design process. Either you started with freehand sketching, and then at a certain point transferred the information to a computer for construction documents, Or some designers simply started out using computer-aided design (CAD). Each method has its advantages and disadvantages. Freehand sketching is more loose and creative, but less accurate. CAD is more accurate, but it is tighter and mathematical, therefore less free and intuitive.

Today you can combine freehand sketches with 3D CAD drawings through the use of a program called SketchUp. Then you can put them together in a presentation by the use of Photoshop or Illustrator. Until recently, using CAD meant investing in a fairly expensive system and training to learn the skills, and most of the emphasis was on 2D drafting.

Beginning around 2000, the SketchUp program became widely available. It was originally tagged "3D for everybody" and offered as a free download. This is the main distinction between SketchUp and other CAD programs. It allows the designer to draw directly in 3D with the same accuracy as other CAD programs—and it's free! It's also very easy to learn, with its own included tutorials and a large library of downloadable furniture.

In 2006, Google bought SketchUp and offered it, still for free, to go along with its own 3D mapping system. SketchUp can be successfully combined with Google Earth to show real-life views of sites in 3D. In 2012, Google sold SketchUp to Trimble, but it continues to be offered as a free download.

Projects in this book have been developed using SketchUp 2014. (There is very little change to SketchUp 2015.) We used SketchUp Pro to develop a "Terrain Model", but nowhere else. The Pro version is more useful for construction documents and import of AutoCad drawings, but it is not appropriate for the design scope of this book.

We used Photoshop CS 4 for the Photoshop instructions. Instructors and students may choose to update to the latest versions prior to their work. Although there may be some minor differences, the principles remain the same.

Computer-Aided Design: A Brief Chronology
AutoCad Chronology

Official Name	Version	Release	Date of release	Comments
AutoCAD Version 1.0	1.0	1	1982, December	DWG R1.0 file format introduced.
AutoCAD Version 1.2	1.2	2	1983, April	DWG R1.2 file format introduced.
AutoCAD Version 1.3	1.3	3	1983, August	DWG R1.3 file format introduced.
AutoCAD Version 1.4	1.4	4	1983, October	DWG R1.4 file format introduced.
AutoCAD Version 2.0	2.0	5	1984, October	DWG R2.05 file format introduced.
AutoCAD Version 2.1	2.1	6	1985, May	DWG R2.1 file format introduced.
AutoCAD Version 2.5	2.5	7	1986, June	DWG R2.5 file format introduced.
AutoCAD Version 2.6	2.6	8	1987, April	DWG R2.6 file format introduced. Last version to run without a math co-processor.
AutoCAD Release 9	9.0	9	1987, September	DWG R9 file format introduced.
AutoCAD Release 10	10.0	10	1988, October	DWG R10 file format introduced.
AutoCAD Release 11	11.0	11	1990, October	DWG R11 file format introduced.
AutoCAD Release 12	12.0	12	1992, June	DWG R11/R12 file format introduced. Last release for Apple Macintosh till 2010.
AutoCAD Release 13	13.0	13	1994, November	DWG R13 file format introduced. Last release for Unix, MS-DOS and Windows 3.11.
AutoCAD Release 14	14.0	14	1997, February	DWG R14 file format introduced.
AutoCAD 2000	15.0	15	1999, March	DWG 2000 file format introduced.
AutoCAD 2000i	15.1	16	2000, July	
AutoCAD 2002	15.6	17	2001, June	
AutoCAD 2004	16.0	18	2003, March	DWG 2004 file format introduced.
AutoCAD 2005	16.1	19	2004, March	
AutoCAD 2006	16.2	20	2005, March	
AutoCAD 2007	17.0	21	2006, March	DWG 2007 file format introduced.
AutoCAD 2008	17.1	22	2007, March	Annotative Objects introduced. First release for the x86-64 versions of Windows XP and Vista.
AutoCAD 2009	17.2	23	2008, March	Revisions to the user interface including the option of a Microsoft Office 2007-like tabbed ribbon.
AutoCAD 2010	18.0	24	2009, March 24	DWG 2010 file format introduced. Parametrics introduced. Mesh 3D solid modeling introduced. Both 32-bit and 64-bit versions of AutoCAD 2010 and AutoCAD LT 2010 are compatible with and supported under Microsoft Windows 7.
AutoCAD 2011	18.1	25	2010, March 25	Surface Modeling, Surface Analysis and Object Transparency introduced. October 15, 2010[5] AutoCAD 2011 for Mac was released. Are compatible with and supported under Microsoft Windows 7
AutoCAD 2012	18.2	26	2011, March 22	Associative Array, Model Documentation
AutoCAD 2013	19.0	27	2012, March 27	DWG 2013 file format introduced.

Narrative Notes

File Formats

The native file format of AutoCAD is *.dwg*. This and, to a lesser extent, its interchange file format *DXF*, have become de facto, if proprietary, standards for CAD data interoperability. AutoCAD has included support for .dwg, a format developed and promoted by Autodesk, for publishing CAD data. In 2006, Autodesk estimated the number of active .dwg files at in excess of one billion. In the past, Autodesk has estimated the total number of existing .dwg files as more than three billion.

History

AutoCAD was derived from a program called Interact, which was written in a proprietary language (SPL) by inventor Michael Riddle. This early version ran on the Marinchip Systems 9900 computer. (Marinchip Systems was owned by Autodesk co-founders John Walker and Dan Drake.) Walker paid Riddle US$10 million for the CAD technology.

When Marinchip Software Partners (later known as Autodesk) formed, the co-founders decided to re-code Interact in C and PL/1. They chose C because it seemed to be the biggest upcoming language. In the end, the PL/1 version was unsuccessful. The C version was, at the time, one of the most complex programs in that language. Autodesk had to work with a compiler developer, Lattice, to update C, enabling AutoCAD to run. Early releases of AutoCAD used primitive entities (e.g., lines, polylines, circles, arcs, and text) to construct more complex objects. Since the mid-1990s, AutoCAD supported custom objects through its C++ Application Programming Interface (API).

The modern AutoCAD includes a full set of basic solid modeling and 3D tools. The release of AutoCAD 2007 included the improved 3D modeling that provided better navigation when working in 3D. Moreover, it became easier to edit 3D models. The mental ray engine was included in rendering, and therefore it is possible to do quality renderings. AutoCAD 2010 introduced parametric functionality and mesh modeling.

1992–2010 For use on PCs only

2010 3D modeling introduced

(Citations above from http://en.wikipedia.org/wiki/AutoCAD#History)

Meanwhile, Macintosh Computer began its own series of CAD drawing programs. The SketchUp program was then introduced in 1999. Following are some dates:

1984   **MacDraw** was a vector-based drawing application released along with the first Apple Macintosh systems in 1984. MacDraw was one of the first WYSIWYG drawing programs that could be used in collaboration with MacWrite. MacDraw was useful for drawing technical diagrams and floorplans. It was eventually adapted by Claris and, in the early 1990s, MacDraw Pro was released with color support. MacDraw is the vector edition of MacPaint.

(Citations above from http://en.wikipedia.org/wiki/MacDraw)

1986   **ArchiCad**

1986   First version with integrated 2D/3D

1987   First color version

(Citations above from http://www.archicadwiki.com/ArchiCAD%20 versions)

1999   **SketchUp-Initial development**

SketchUp was developed by startup company @Last Software of Boulder, Colorado, co-founded in 1999 by Brad Schell and Joe Esch. SketchUp debuted in August 2000 as a general-purpose 3D content-creation tool, with the tagline "3D for everyone." Its creators envisioned a software program "that would allow design professionals to draw the way they want by emulating the feel and freedom of working with pen and paper in a simple and elegant interface, that would be fun to use and easy to learn, and that would be used by designers to play with their designs in a way that is not possible with traditional design software. It also has user-friendly buttons to make it easier to use.[1]

(Citations above from http://en.wikipedia.org/wiki/SketchUp)

---

1. In April 2012, Google sold SketchUp to Trimble, but for the near future it will continue to be a free download. See the following article for more information: http://www.sensysmag.com/spatialsustain/why-did-trimble-buy-sketchup-and-why-did-google-sell.html.

Emergency Shelters and Sustainable Use

Architects and designers can have a central role in this continuous process of healing and changing before, during, or in the aftermath of catastrophes. They can design emergency shelters that are sound and can be built before there is an actual emergency. These shelters can be placed in sustainable locations (such as not in floodplains), where they can be of immediate use in case of an emergency. The shelters can also remain in place after the emergency has passed, rather than be destroyed and added to a landfill, as temporary residences have been in the past.

By quickly communicating their ideas through sketches and 3D digital models, designers can provide valuable information to other groups that are also interested in solving these problems, but who might not easily read plans. Sharing of ideas through digital images can help those in the fields of health care, transportation, education, agriculture, and employment visualize the structures planned and thereby help them implement common goals for the community.

It would be better if these disasters never happened, but because they have and they no doubt will continue, let us find the thinking and the means to use it to make our architecture and social life as good as or better than before.

Appendix B demonstrates that the designers, using new digital tools, can provide valuable input to other members of the community. They can help improve damaged environments even before there is a crisis, which will then hold their value once the crisis has passed.

Emergency/Multipurpose House*

This type of dwelling could be used in emergency situations, but it would remain after the crisis abates. It could also be a starter for a larger house. Nothing is wasted: It is 150 square feet, with combined living, dining, kitchen, and sleeping areas. A compact toilet with boat shower is also included. This multipurpose house could also be used as a mother- or father-in-law space, a room for a returning adult child, or a rental unit.

---

*The idea for this type of structure came from my graduate student Daniel Heckman for his thesis project.

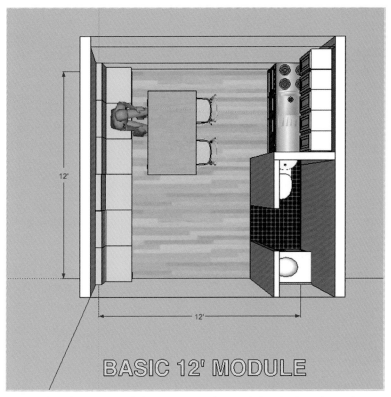

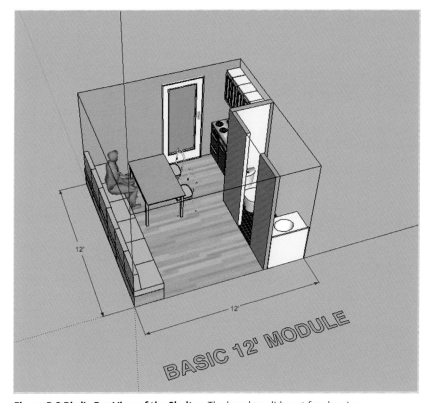

Figure B.1 Plan of emergency shelter, 150 square feet, including kitchen, dining, living, sleeping, and shower areas. The shower is a "boat shower" in the lavatory.

Figure B.2 Bird's-Eye View of the Shelter. The benches slide out for sleeping.

Sandbox Tool

In some emergency situations, like where you may want to raise new terrain above the flood plain, you can use the **Sandbox** tool. We may choose to use the Sandbox tool to show contours in the landscape, such as Patrick Rosen did in the Gallery example of his Dunes House in **Chapter 12**. Sandbox is included in the free SketchUp download, but you have to specifically activate those tools. From the SketchUp icon pull-down tab, go to **Preferences**. A box opens up with **Extension Options**. Scroll down and check the box next to **Sandbox** tools.

Step-By-Step

1. First, set **Preferences>Extensions>Sandbox Tools>From Scratch>Grid Spacing**, say to 10 feet (depends on size of area).
2. Then **Edit>Edit Group>Explode>** the grid.
3. Select an area on the grid and click or triple-click (not sure which works best). This will activate that portion of the grid with yellow grips that can be moved individually.
4. Use the **Move** tool to grab parts for modeling the various heights.
5. Right-click **Smooth>Soften building edge or Co-Planar.**

(If you are importing a jpeg to the Sandbox, you might want to "explode" the image to allow the Sandbox contours to "pass through" it.)

Figure B.3 The Dunes House by Patrick Rosen (also shown in **Chapter 12**) is an example of how to use the Sandbox tool.

This book is intended to be a new tool for a new time in design and design representation. It has presented three separate rendering techniques—freehand drawing, SketchUp, and Photoshop—and shown how these different techniques can all be integrated and used where they can do the most good in interior design. Until quite recently, the idea of integrating these hand and digital methods was controversial. Many designers were strongly committed to one or the other technique to such an extent that there were camps and schools of thought. What happened to change that? The spirit and language of designer/client relations has changed. We live in a period in which professionals—practitioners of different sorts—willingly seek to expand the collaborative environment.

The tools you have learned in this book will be very useful for a true collaborative team effort to solve community-wide problems. Sharing of plans through 3D digital images can help designers share their work with others in the fields of health care, transportation, education, agriculture, and employment. They will all be able to more easily visualize images and, therefore, how they relate to each other in different spaces and environments.

Integrating hand and digital languages is a significant way this is happening in the design studios and client meetings. As designers, you will be in the business of communicating visual ideas that can easily seem abstract and incomprehensible to nonspecialists. By integrating 3D rendering techniques—bringing the hand and keyboard/screen together in this process—we are seeing good results and satisfying conclusions to design projects.

Integrating drawing techniques is an important way we attempt to make the design conversation larger and more inclusive than ever. Welcome to the profession!

INDEX

Please note that page numbers in bold indicate defined terms; page numbers with *f* indicate figures; page numbers with *n* indicate footnotes.